CliffsN

Brontë's
Jane Eyre

By Karin Jacobson, Ph.D.

IN THIS BOOK

- Learn about the Life and Background of the Author

- Preview and Introduction to the Novel

- Explore themes, character development, and recurring images in the Critical Commentaries

- Examine in-depth Character Analyses

- Acquire an understanding of the novel with Critical Essays

- Reinforce what you learn with CliffsNotes Review

- Find additional information to further your study in the CliffsNotes Resource Center and online at www.cliffsnotes.com

IDG Books Worldwide, Inc.
An International Data Group Company
Foster City, CA • Chicago, IL • Indianapolis, IN • New York, NY

About the Author

Karin Jacobson received her Ph.D. in English from The Ohio State University and currently teaches English and Composition at the University of Minnesota-Duluth.

Publisher's Acknowledgments

Editorial

Project Editor: Tere Drenth

Acquisitions Editor: Greg Tubach

Editorial Administrator: Michelle Hacker

Glossary Editors: The editors and staff of Webster's New World Dictionaries

Production

Indexer: York Production Services, Inc.

Proofreader: York Production Services, Inc.

IDG Books Indianapolis Production Department

CliffsNotes™ Brontë's *Jane Eyre*

Published by

IDG Books Worldwide, Inc.

An International Data Group Company

919 E. Hillsdale Blvd.

Suite 400

Foster City, CA 94404

www.idgbooks.com (IDG Books Worldwide Web site)

www.cliffsnotes.com (CliffsNotes Web site)

ISBN: 0-7645-8589-4

Printed in the United States of America

10 9 8 7 6 5 4 3 2 1

1O/QR/QW/QQ/IN

Distributed in the United States by IDG Books Worldwide, Inc.

Library of Congress Cataloging-in-Publication Data

Jacobson, Ph.D., Karin.

CliffsNotes Brontë's Jane Eyre / Karin Jacobson, Ph.D.

p. cm.

Includes index.

ISBN 0-7645-8589-4 (alk. paper)

1. Brontë, Charlotte, 1816-1855. Jane Eyre--Examinations--Study guides. I. Title: Jane Eyre. II. Title

PR4167.J5 J34 2000

823'.8--dc21   00-0038846

CIP

Distributed by CDG Books Canada Inc. for Canada; by Transworld Publishers Limited in the United Kingdom; by IDG Norge Books for Norway; by IDG Sweden Books for Sweden; by IDG Books Australia Publishing Corporation Pty. Ltd. for Australia and New Zealand; by Trans Quest Publishers Pte Ltd. for Singapore, Malaysia, Thailand, Indonesia, and Hong Kong; by Gotop Information Inc. for Taiwan; by ICG Muse, Inc. for Japan; by Intersoft for South Africa; by Eyrolles for France; by International Thomson Publishing for Germany, Austria and Switzerland; by Distribuidora Cuspide for Argentina; by LR International for Brazil; by Galileo Libros for Chile; by Ediciones ZETA S.C.R. Ltda. for Peru; by WS Computer Publishing Corporation, Inc., for the Philippines; by Contemporanea de Ediciones for Venezuela; by Express Computer Distributors for the Caribbean and West Indies; by Micronesia Media Distributor, Inc. for Micronesia; by Chips Computadoras S.A. de C.V. for Mexico; by Editorial Norma de Panama S.A. for Panama; by American Bookshops for Finland.

For general information on IDG Books Worldwide's books in the U.S., please call our Consumer Customer Service department at **800-762-2974.** For reseller information, including discounts and premium sales, please call our Reseller Customer Service department at **800-434-3422.**

For information on where to purchase IDG Books Worldwide's books outside the U.S., please contact our International Sales department at **317-596-5530** or fax **317-572-4002.**

For consumer information on foreign language translations, please contact our Customer Service department at **800-434-3422,** fax 317-572-4002, or e-mail rights@idgbooks.com.

For information on licensing foreign or domestic rights, please phone **650-653-7098.**

For sales inquiries and special prices for bulk quantities, please contact our Order Services department at **800-434-3422** or write to the address above.

For information on using IDG Books Worldwide's books in the classroom or for ordering examination copies, please contact our Educational Sales department at **800-434-2086** or fax **317-572-4005.**

For press review copies, author interviews, or other publicity information, please contact our Public Relations department at **650-653-7000** or fax **650-653-7500.**

For authorization to photocopy items for corporate, personal, or educational use, please contact Copyright Clearance Center, 222 Rosewood Drive, Danvers, MA 01923, or fax **978-750-4470.**

Table of Contents

How to Use This Book

CliffsNotes *Jane Eyre* supplements the original work, giving you background information about the author, an introduction to the novel, a graphical character map, critical commentaries, expanded glossaries, and a comprehensive index. CliffsNotes Review tests your comprehension of the original text and reinforces learning with questions and answers, practice projects, and more. For further information on Charlotte Brontë and *Jane Eyre*, check out the CliffsNotes Resource Center.

CliffsNotes provides the following icons to highlight essential elements of particular interest:

Reveals the underlying themes in the work.

Helps you to more easily relate to or discover the depth of a character.

Uncovers elements such as setting, atmosphere, mystery, passion, violence, irony, symbolism, tragedy, foreshadowing, and satire.

Enables you to appreciate the nuances of words and phrases.

Don't Miss Our Web Site

Discover classic literature as well as modern-day treasures by visiting the Cliffs-Notes Web site at www.cliffsnotes.com. You can obtain a quick download of a CliffsNotes title, purchase a title in print form, browse our catalog, or view online samples.

You'll also find interactive tools that are fun and informative, links to interesting Web sites, tips, articles, and additional resources to help you, not only for literature, but for test prep, finance, careers, computers, and the Internet, too. See you at www.cliffsnotes.com!

LIFE AND BACKGROUND OF THE AUTHOR

Personal Background

At age twenty, Charlotte Brontë sent a sample of her poetry to England's Poet Laureate, Robert Southey. His comments urged her to abandon all literary pursuits: "Literature cannot be the business of a woman's life, and it ought not to be. The more she is engaged in her proper duties, the less leisure will she have for it, even as an accomplishment and a recreation." His response indicates the political difficulties women faced as they tried to enter the literary arena in Victorian England; domestic responsibilities were expected to require all their energy, leaving no time for creative pursuits. Despite a lack of support from the outside world, Charlotte Brontë found sufficient internal motivation and enthusiasm from her sisters to become a successful writer and balance her familial and creative needs.

Born at Thornton, Yorkshire on April 21, 1816, Charlotte was the third child of Patrick Brontë and Maria Branwell. In 1820, her father received a curate post in Haworth, a remote town on the Yorkshire moors, where Charlotte spent most of her life. In 1821, Mrs. Brontë died from what was thought to be cancer. Charlotte and her four sisters, Maria, Elizabeth, Emily and Anne, and their brother, Branwell, were raised primarily by their unpleasant, maiden aunt, Elizabeth Branwell, who provided them with little supervision. Not only were the children free to roam the moors, but their father allowed them to read whatever interested them: Shakespeare, *The Arabian Nights*, *Pilgrim's Progress*, and the poems of Byron were some of their favorites.

When a school for the daughters of poor clergymen opened at Cowan Bridge in 1824, Mr. Brontë decided to send his oldest four daughters there to receive a formal education. Most biographers argue that Charlotte's description of Lowood School in *Jane Eyre* accurately reflects the dismal conditions at this school. Charlotte's two oldest sisters, Maria and Elizabeth, died in 1824 of tuberculosis they contracted due to the poor management of the school. Following this tragedy, Patrick Brontë withdrew Charlotte and Emily from Cowan Bridge.

Grieving over their sisters' deaths and searching for a way to alleviate their loneliness, the remaining four siblings began writing a series of stories, *The Glass-Town*, stimulated by a set of toy soldiers their father had given them. In these early writings, the children collaboratively created a complete imaginary world, a fictional West African empire they called Angria. Charlotte explained their interest in writing this way: "We were wholly dependent on ourselves and each other, on books and study, for the enjoyments and occupations of life. The highest stimulus, as well as the liveliest pleasure we had know from childhood upwards, lay in attempts at literary composition." Through her early twenties, Charlotte routinely revised and expanded pieces of the Angria story, developing several key characters and settings. While this writing helped Charlotte improve her literary style, the Angria adventures are fantastical, melodramatic, and repetitive, contrasting with Charlotte's more realistic adult fiction.

After her father had a dangerous lung disorder, he decided once again that his daughters should receive an education so they would be assured of an income if he died. In 1831, Charlotte entered the Misses Wooler's school at Roe Head. Shy and solitary, Charlotte was not happy at school, but she still managed to win several academic awards and to make two lifelong friends: Mary Taylor and Ellen Nussey. Although she was offered a teaching job at Roe Head, Charlotte declined the position, choosing to return to Haworth instead. Perhaps bored with the solitary life at Haworth and looking for an active occupation in the world, Charlotte returned to Roe Head in 1835 as a governess. For her, governessing was akin to "slavery," because she felt temperamentally unsuited for it, and finally, following a near mental breakdown in 1838, she was forced to resign her position. Unfortunately, governessing was the only real employment opportunity middle-class women had in Victorian England. Because the family needed the money, Charlotte suffered through two more unhappy governess positions, feeling like an unappreciated servant in wealthy families' homes; she didn't enjoy living in other people's houses because it caused "estrangement from one's real character."

In an attempt to create a job that would allow her to maintain her independence, Charlotte formed the idea of starting her own school at Haworth. To increase her teaching qualifications before beginning this venture, she enrolled as a student, at the age of twenty-six, at the Pensionnat Heger in Brussels so she could increase her fluency in French and learn German. Charlotte loved the freedom and adventure of living in a new culture, and formed an intense, though one-sided, passion for the married headmaster at the school: Monsieur Heger. After two years in Brussels, suffering perhaps from her love for Heger, Charlotte returned to England. The plan to open her own school was a failure, as she was unable to attract a single student.

Instead, Charlotte began putting all of her energy into her writing. After discovering Emily's poems, Charlotte decided that she, Anne, and

Emily should try to publish a collection of poems at their own expense. In 1846, they accomplished this goal, using the masculine pseudonyms of Currer, Acton, and Ellis Bell because of the double standards against women authors. Although their book, *Poems*, was not a financial success, the women continued their literary endeavors. Excited to be writing full-time, they each began a novel. Anne's *Agnes Grey* and Emily's *Wuthering Heights* both found publishers, but Charlotte's somewhat autobiographical account of her experiences in Brussels, *The Professor*, was rejected by several publishers. Again refusing to become discouraged, Charlotte began writing *Jane Eyre* in 1846, while on a trip to Manchester with her father where he was undergoing cataract surgery. While he convalesced, Charlotte wrote. The firm of Smith, Elder, and Company agreed to publish the resulting novel, and the first edition of *Jane Eyre* was released on October 16, 1847. The novel was an instant success, launching Charlotte into literary fame. It also netted her an impressive 500 pounds, twenty-five times her salary as a governess.

But the pleasures of literary success were soon overshadowed by family tragedy. In 1848, after Anne and Charlotte had revealed the true identity of the "Bells" to their publishers, their brother Branwell died. Never living up to his family's high expectations for him, Branwell died an opium-addicted, debauched, alcoholic failure. Emily and Anne died soon after. Although Charlotte completed her second novel, *Shirley* in 1849, her sadness at the loss of her remaining siblings left her emotionally shattered. She became a respected member of the literary community only when her sisters, her most enthusiastic supporters, were no longer able to share her victory. Visiting London following the publication of this book, Charlotte became acquainted with several important writers, including William Thackeray and Elizabeth Gaskell, who was to write Charlotte's biography following her death.

In 1852, the Reverend Arthur B. Nicholls, Mr. Brontë's curate at Haworth beginning in 1845, proposed marriage to Charlotte. Earlier in her life, Charlotte had rejected several marriage proposals because she was hoping to discover true love, but loneliness following the death of her last three siblings may have led her to accept Nicholls' proposal. Saying she had "esteem" but not love for Nicholls, Charlotte's relationship with her husband was certainly not the overwhelming passion of Jane and Rochester. Her father's jealous opposition to the marriage led Charlotte initially to reject Nicholls, who left Haworth in 1853, the year *Villette* was published. By 1854, Reverend Brontë's opposition to the union had abated somewhat, and the ceremony was performed on

June 29, 1854. After the marriage, Charlotte had little time for writing, as she was forced to perform the duties expected of a minister's wife and take care of her aging father. In 1854 Charlotte, in the early stages of pregnancy, caught pneumonia while on a long, rain-drenched walk on the moors. She died on March 31, 1855, a month before her thirty-ninth birthday. *The Professor*, written in 1846 and 1847, was posthumously published in 1857, along with Mrs. Gaskell's *Life of Charlotte Brontë*.

INTRODUCTION TO THE NOVEL

Introduction

When *Jane Eyre* was first published in 1847, it was an immediate popular and critical success. George Lewes, a famous Victorian literary critic declared it "the best novel of the season." It also, however, met with criticism. In a famous attack in the *Quarterly Review* of December 1848, Elizabeth Rigby called Jane a "personification of an unregenerate and undisciplined spirit" and the novel as a whole, "anti-Christian." Rigby's critique perhaps accounts for some of the novel's continuing popularity: the rebelliousness of its tone. *Jane Eyre* calls into question most of society's major institutions, including education, family, social class, and Christianity. The novel asks the reader to consider a variety of contemporary social and political issues: What is women's position in society, what is the relation between Britain and its colonies, how important is artistic endeavor in human life, what is the relationship of dreams and fantasy to reality, and what is the basis of an effective marriage? Although the novel poses all of these questions, it doesn't didactically offer a single answer to any of them. Readers can construct their own answers, based on their unique and personal analyses of the book. This multidimensionality makes *Jane Eyre* a novel that rewards multiple readings.

While the novel's longevity resides partially in its social message, posing questions still relevant to twenty-first century readers, its combination of literary genre keeps the story entertaining and enjoyable. Not just the story of the romance between Rochester and Jane, the novel also employs the conventions of the bildungsroman (a novel that shows the psychological or moral development of its main character), the gothic and the spiritual quest. As bildungsroman, the first-person narration plots Jane's growth from an isolated and unloved orphan into a happily married, independent woman. Jane's appeals to the reader directly involve us in this journey of self-knowledge; the reader becomes her accomplice, learning and changing along with the heroine. The novel's gothic element emphasizes the supernatural, the visionary, and the horrific. Mr. Reed's ghostly presence in the red-room, Bertha's strange laughter at Thornfield, and Rochester's dark and brooding persona are all examples of gothic conventions, which add to the novel's suspense, entangling the reader in Jane's attempt to solve the mystery at Thornfield. Finally, the novel could also be read as a spiritual quest, as Jane tries to position herself in relationship to religion at each stop on her journey. Although she paints a negative picture of the established religious community through her characterizations of Mr. Brocklehurst,

St. John Rivers, and Eliza Reed, Jane finds an effective, personal perspective on religion following her night on the moors. For her, when one is closest to nature, one is also closest to God: "We read clearest His infinitude, His omnipotence, His omnipresence." God and nature are both sources of bounty, compassion and forgiveness.

In reading this novel, consider keeping a reading journal, writing down quotes that spark your interest. When you've finished the book, return to these notes and group your quotes under specific categories. For example, you may list all quotes related to governesses. Based on these quotes, what seems to be the novel's overall message about governesses? Do different characters have conflicting perceptions of governesses? Which character's ideas does the novel seem to sympathize with and why? Do you agree with the novel's message? By looking at the novel closely and reading it with a critical focus, you will enrich your own reading experience, joining the readers over the last century who've been excited by plain Jane's journey of self-discovery.

A Brief Synopsis

Orphaned as an infant, Jane Eyre lives with at Gateshead with her aunt, Sarah Reed, as the novel opens. Jane is ten years old, an outsider in the Reed family. Her female cousins, Georgiana and Eliza, tolerate, but don't love her. Their brother, John, is more blatantly hostile to Jane, reminding her that she is a poor dependent of his mother who shouldn't even be associating with the children of a gentleman. One day he is angered to find Jane reading one of his books, so he takes the book away and throws it at her. Finding this treatment intolerable, Jane fights back. She is blamed for the conflagration and sent to the red-room, the place where her kind Uncle Reed died. In this frightening room, Jane thinks she sees her uncle's ghost and begs to be set free. Her Aunt Reed refuses, insisting Jane remain in her prison until she learns complete submissiveness. When the door to the red-room is locked once again, Jane passes out. She wakes back in her own room, with the kind physician, Mr. Lloyd, standing over her bed. He advises Aunt Reed to send Jane away to school, because she is obviously unhappy at Gateshead.

Jane is sent to Lowood School, a charity institution for orphan girls, run by Mr. Brocklehurst. A stingy and mean-hearted minister, Brocklehurst provides the girls with starvation levels of food, freezing rooms, and poorly made clothing and shoes. He justifies his poor treatment of them by saying that they need to learn humility and by comparing them to the Christian martyrs, who also endured great hardships. Despite the difficult conditions at Lowood, Jane prefers school to life with the Reeds. Here she makes two new friends: Miss Temple and Helen Burns. From Miss Temple, Jane learns proper ladylike behavior and compassion; from Helen she gains a more spiritual focus. The school's damp conditions, combined with the girls' near-starvation diet, produces a typhus epidemic, in which nearly half the students die, including Helen Burns, who dies in Jane's arms. Following this tragedy, Brocklehurst is deposed from his position as manager of Lowood, and conditions become more acceptable. Jane quickly becomes a star student, and after six years of hard work, an effective teacher. Following two years of teaching at Lowood, Jane is ready for new challenges. Miss Temple marries, and Lowood seems different without her. Jane places at advertisement for a governess position in the local newspaper. She receives only one reply, from a Mrs. Fairfax of Thornfield, near Millcote, who seeks a governess for a ten-year old girl. Jane accepts the job.

At Thornfield, a comfortable three-story country estate, Jane is warmly welcomed. She likes both her new pupil, Adèle Varens, and Mrs. Fairfax, the housekeeper at Thornfield, but is soon restless. One January afternoon, while walking to Millcote to mail a letter, Jane helps a horseman whose horse has slipped on a patch of ice and fallen. Returning to Thornfield, Jane discovers that this man is Edward Fairfax Rochester, the owner of Thornfield and her employer. He is a dark-haired, moody man in his late thirties. Although he is often taciturn, Jane grows fond of his mysterious, passionate nature. He tells Jane about Adèle's mother, Céline, a Parisian opera-singer who was once his mistress. Adèle, he claims, is not his daughter, but he rescued the poor girl after her mother abandoned her.

Jane also discovers that Thornfield harbors a secret. From time to time, she hears strange, maniacal laughter coming from the third story. Mrs. Fairfax claims this is just Grace Poole, an eccentric servant with a drinking problem. But Jane wonders if this is true. One night, Jane smells smoke in the hallway, and realizes it is coming from Rochester's room. Jane races down to his room, discovering his curtains and bed are on fire. Unable to wake Rochester, she douses both him and his bedding with cold water. He asks her not to tell anyone about this incident and blames the arson on Grace Poole. Why doesn't he press charges on Grace, or at least evict her from the house, Jane wonders.

Following this incident, Rochester leaves suddenly for a house party at a local estate. Jane is miserable during his absence and realizes she is falling in love with him. After a weeklong absence, he returns with a party of guests, including the beautiful Blanche Ingram. Jane jealously believes Rochester is pursing this accomplished, majestic, dark-haired beauty. An old friend of Rochester's, Richard Mason, joins the party one day. From him, Jane learns that Rochester once lived in Spanish Town, Jamaica. One night, Mason is mysteriously attacked, supposedly by the crazy Grace Poole.

Jane leaves Thornfield for a month to attend her aunt, who is on her deathbed following her son John's excessive debauchery and apparent suicide. Jane tries to create a reconciliation with her aunt, but the woman refuses all Jane's attempts at appeasement. Before dying, she gives Jane a letter from her uncle, John Eyre, who had hoped to adopt Jane and make her his heir. The letter was sent three years ago, but Aunt Reed had vindictively kept it from Jane. Sarah Reed dies, unloved by her daughters.

When Jane returns to Thornfield, the houseguests have left. Rochester tells Jane he will soon marry Blanche, so she and Adèle will need to leave Thornfield. In the middle of this charade, Jane reveals her love for him, and the two end up engaged. Jane is happy to be marrying the man she loves, but during the month before the wedding she is plagued by strange dreams of a destroyed Thornfield and a wailing infant. Two nights before the wedding, a frightening, dark-haired woman enters her room and rips her wedding veil in two. Although Jane is certain this woman didn't look like Grace Poole, Rochester assures her it must have been the bizarre servant. The morning of the wedding finally arrives. Jane and Rochester stand at the altar, taking their vows, when suddenly a strange man announces there's an impediment to the marriage: Rochester is already married to a woman named Bertha Antoinetta Mason. Rochester rushes the wedding party back to Thornfield, where they find his insane and repulsive wife locked in a room on the third story. Grace Poole is the woman's keeper, but Bertha was responsible for the strange laughter and violence at Thornfield. Rochester tries to convince Jane to become his mistress and move with him to a pleasure villa in the south of France.

Instead, Jane sneaks away in the middle of the night, with little money and no extra clothing. With twenty shillings, the only money she has, she catches a coach that takes her to faraway Whitcross. There, she spends three days roaming the woods, looking for work and, finally, begging for food. On the third night, she follows a light that leads her across the moors to Marsh End (also called Moor House), owned by the Rivers family. Hannah, the housekeeper, wants to send her away, but St. John Rivers, the clergyman who owns the house, offers her shelter. Jane soon becomes close friends with St. John's sisters, Diana and Mary, and he offers Jane a humble job as the schoolmistress for the poor girls in his parish at Morton. Because their father lost most of his money before he died, Diana and Mary have been forced to earn a living by working as governesses.

One day, St. John learns that, unbeknownst to her, Jane has inherited 20,000 pounds from her uncle, John Eyre. Furthermore, she discovers that St. John's real name is St. John Eyre Rivers, so he, his sisters, and Jane are cousins. The Rivers were cut out of John Eyre's will because of an argument between John and their father. Thrilled to discover that she has a family, Jane insists on splitting the inheritance four ways, and then remodels Moor House for her cousins, who will no longer need to work as governesses. Not content with his life as a smalltime clergyman, St. John plans to become a missionary in India. He tries to convince Jane to accompany him, as his wife. Realizing that St. John doesn't love her but just wants to use her to accomplish his goals, Jane refuses his request, but suggests a compromise by agreeing to follow him to India as a comrade, but not as a wife. St. John tries to coerce her into the marriage, and has almost succeeded, when, one night Jane suddenly hears Rochester's disembodied voice calling out to her.

Jane leaves Moor House to search for her true love, Rochester. Arriving at Millcote, she discovers Thornfield a burned wreck, just as predicted in her dreams. From a local innkeeper, she learns that Bertha Mason burned the house down one night and that Rochester lost an eye and a hand while trying to save her and the servants. He now lives in seclusion at Ferndean.

Jane immediately drives to Ferndean. There she discovers a powerless, unhappy Rochester. Jane carries a tray to him and reveals her identity. The two lovers are joyfully reunited and soon marry. Ten years later, Jane writes this narrative. Her married life is still blissful; Adèle has grown to be a helpful companion for Jane; Diana and Mary Rivers are happily married; St. John still works as a missionary, but is nearing death; and Rochester has regained partial vision, enough to see their first-born son.

List of Characters

Jane Eyre The orphaned protagonist of the story. When the novel begins, she is an isolated, powerless ten-year-old living with an aunt and cousins who dislike her. As the novel progresses, she grows in strength. She distinguishes herself at Lowood School because of her hard work and strong intellectual abilities. As a governess at Thornfield, she learns of the pleasures and pains of love through her relationship with Edward Rochester. After being deceived by him, she goes to Marsh End, where she regains her spiritual focus and discovers her own strength when she rejects St. John River's marriage proposal. By novel's end she has become a powerful, independent woman, blissfully married to the man she loves, Rochester.

Edward Fairfax Rochester Jane's lover; a dark, passionate, brooding man. A traditional romantic hero, Rochester has lived a troubled life. Married to an insane Creole woman, Bertha Mason, Rochester sought solace for several years in the arms of mistresses. Finally, he seeks to purify his life and wants Jane Eyre, the innocent governess he has hired to teach his foster daughter, Adèle Varens, to become his wife. The wedding falls through when she learns of the existence of his wife. As penance for his transgressions, he is punished by the loss of an eye and a hand when Bertha sets fire to Thornfield. He finally gains happiness at the novel's end when he is reunited with Jane.

Sarah Reed Jane's unpleasant aunt, who raises her until she is ten years old. Despite Jane's attempts at reconciliation before her aunt's death, her aunt refuses to relent. She dies unloved by her children and unrepentant of her mistreatment of Jane.

John Reed Jane's nasty and spoiled cousin, responsible for Jane's banishment to the red-room. Addicted to drinking and gambling, John supposedly commits suicide at the age of twenty-three when his mother is no longer willing or able to pay his debts.

Eliza Reed Another one of Jane's spoiled cousins, Eliza is insanely jealous of the beauty of her sister, Georgiana. She nastily breaks up

Georgiana's elopement with Lord Edwin Vere, and then becomes a devout Christian. But her brand of Christianity is devoid of all compassion or humanity; she shows no sympathy for her dying mother and vows to break off all contact with Georgiana after their mother's death. Usefulness is her mantra. She enters a convent in Lisle, France, eventually becoming the Mother Superior and leaving her money to the church.

Georgiana Reed Eliza's and John's sister, Georgiana is the beauty of the family. She's also shallow and self-centered, interested primarily in her own pleasure. She accuses her sister, Eliza, of sabotaging her plans to marry Lord Edwin Vere. Like Eliza, she shows no emotion following their mother's death. Eventually, Georgiana marries a wealthy, but worn-out society man.

Bessie Lee The maid at Gateshead who sometimes consoles Jane by telling her entertaining stories and singing her songs. Bessie visits Jane at Lowood, impressed by Jane's intellectual attainments and ladylike behavior. Bessie marries the coachman, Robert Leaven, and has three children.

Mr. Lloyd The kind apothecary who suggests that Jane be sent to school following her horrifying experience in the red-room. His letter to Miss Temple clears Jane of the accusations Mrs. Reed has made against her.

Mr. Brocklehurst The stingy, mean-hearted manager of Lowood. He hypocritically feeds the girls at the school starvation-level rations, while his wife and daughters live luxuriously. The minister of Brocklebridge Church, he represents a negative brand of Christianity, one that lacks all compassion or kindness.

Helen Burns Jane's spiritual and intellectual friend at Lowood. Although she is unfairly punished by Miss Scatcherd at Lowood, Helen maintains her poise, partially through her loving friendship with Miss Temple. From Helen, Jane learns tolerance and peace, but Jane can't accept Helen's rejection of the material world. Helen's impressive intellectual attainments inspire Jane to work hard at school. Dying in Jane's arms, Helen looks forward to peace in heaven and eventual reunion with Jane.

Maria Temple The warm-hearted superintendent at Lowood who generously offers the girls bread and cheese when their breakfasts are inedible. An impressive scholar, a model of ladylike behavior and a compassionate person, Miss Temple is a positive role model for Jane. She cares for Jane and Helen, offering them seedcake in her room and providing Helen with a warm, private bed when she is dying.

Miss Miller Teacher for the youngest students at Lowood who greets Jane on her first night at the school.

Miss Scatcherd The history and grammar teacher at Lowood. She constantly humiliates and punishes Helen Burns.

Miss Smith A red-cheeked teacher at Lowood who is in charge of sewing instruction.

Madame Pierrot The likeable French teacher at Lowood who comes from Lisle, France.

Miss Gryce Jane's roommate and fellow teacher at Lowood.

Mrs. Alice Fairfax The housekeeper at Thornfield; Jane first thinks she is Thornfield's owner. She warmly welcomes Jane to Thornfield, providing a contrast to Jane's cold treatment at Gateshead, the Reed's house. Mrs. Fairfax doesn't approve of Jane and Rochester's marriage because of the differences in their ages and social classes. When she leaves Thornfield after Jane's mysterious disappearance, Rochester offers her a generous pension.

Blanche Ingram The beautiful and haughty society woman Rochester pretends to love. Her comments about the insipidness of governesses show the lack of respect that most governesses faced in the wealthy Victorian families where they worked. As a fortune-hunter, more interested in Rochester's money than his personality, Blanche is depicted as an unappealingly materialist model of femininity.

Adèle Varens Jane's pupil at Thornfield, whose foreignness, like her mother's, reveals many of Jane's Anglocentric prejudices. Adèle initially shows unpleasantly French (in Jane's opinion) characteristics such as sensuality, materialism, and egocentrism. But a firm British education erases all of these negative characteristics, and by the end of the novel Adèle has become a docile, pleasant companion for Jane.

Céline Varens Once Rochester's mistress, this Parisian opera singer used Rochester for his money, although she actually despised him. Rochester discovers her true feelings when he overhears a conversation between her and one of her other lovers. He immediately breaks off relations with her. She eventually runs away to Italy with a musician, abandoning her daughter, Adèle, whom she claims is Rochester's child. Her hypocrisy, sensuality, and materialism make her another negative mode of femininity.

Bertha Antoinetta Mason Rochester Rochester's wife, the crazy woman in the attic. A Creole woman from Spanish Town, Jamaica, Bertha was betrothed to Rochester by the arrangement of their fathers, who planned to consolidate their wealth. This beautiful and majestic woman disintegrates into debauchery, coarseness, and, eventually, madness soon after their wedding. Bertha's mother was also mad and the novel suggests that Bertha's problems are a maternal inheritance. Following the deaths of his brother and father, Rochester returns to England with Bertha, locking her up in the third story of Thornfield, with Grace Poole as her keeper. She occasionally escapes her imprisonment, perpetrating violence whenever she gets loose. Eventually, she sets fire to Thornfield. Bertha is another example of unsavory foreignness in the novel.

Richard (Dick) Mason Bertha's brother, a weak-willed man. During his visit to Thornfield, he is bitten and stabbed by Bertha when he goes up to her room alone. When he learns of Jane's upcoming wedding to Rochester, he arrives to thwart Rochester's bigamous intentions.

Grace Poole Bertha's keeper at Thornfield who has a predilection for gin. Her alcohol-induced lapses allow Bertha to escape from the third floor and perpetrate various crimes in the house, including the eventual fire that destroys Thornfield and maims Rochester. Grace is initially accused of perpetrating all of Bertha's sins in the household.

Mother Bunches Rochester's alias when he's disguised as a gypsy fortuneteller during a house party at Thornfield.

Hannah The Rivers' elderly housekeeper who initially denies Jane access to Moor House. Jane chastises Hannah for her class prejudices, but she and Jane later become friends.

St. John (pronounced sin'jin) Rivers Jane's cousin, St. John is cold, despotic, excessively zealous. Unhappy with his humble position as the minister at Morton, St. John wants to become a missionary in order to meet his ambitions for power and glory. St. John tries to force Jane to marry him and move to India. Jane resists him, and he spends the rest of his life furthering British colonialism by forcing Christian values on the natives.

Diana and Mary Rivers St. John's sisters and Jane's cousins, Diana and Mary are exemplars of accomplished, benevolent, and intellectual women. Working as governesses, they show the ways intelligent, well-bred women are degraded by their positions in wealthy families. Diana's support of Jane following St. John's marriage proposal helps Jane maintain her independence when faced with his despotism.

Rosamond Oliver The beautiful and flirtatious daughter of a wealthy man in Morton, Rosamond finances the girls' school in Morton. Although she seems to love St. John, she has become engaged to the wealthy Mr. Granby before St. John leaves for India. While St. John is physically attracted to her, he realizes that Rosamond would never be a good wife for him, because of her light-hearted, almost shallow, personality.

Mr. Oliver Rosamond's father and the only wealthy man in Morton. While the Rivers are an ancient and esteemed family, the Olivers have "new money." He approves of St. John's talents, finding him a suitable husband for his daughter, but thinks missionary work is a waste of St. John's intellect.

Mr. Briggs John Eyre's attorney, Briggs prevents Jane's bigamous marriage to Rochester and searches for her following her uncle's death so she can claim her inheritance.

John Eyre Jane's and the Rivers' uncle, John Eyre makes a fortune as a wine merchant in Madeira. Although he plans to adopt Jane, he dies before they ever meet, but leaves his entire fortune—20,000 pounds—to her. He quarreled with Mr. Rivers, and therefore, didn't leave his money to the Rivers children.

Alice Wood Hired by Rosamond Oliver, Alice is an orphan who serves as Jane's assistant at Morton.

The elderly servants who care for Rochester at Ferndean after Thornfield is destroyed by the fire.

Character Map

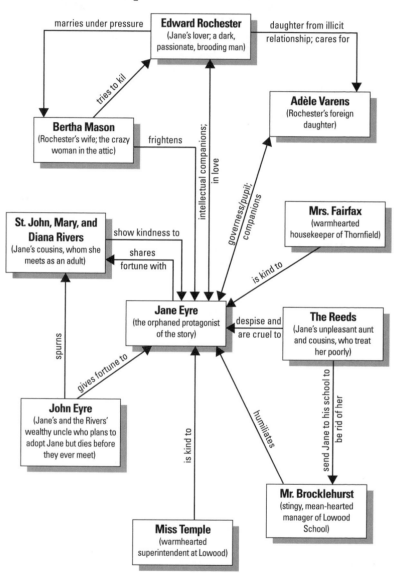

Edward Rochester
(Jane's lover; a dark, passionate, brooding man)

marries under pressure

daughter from illicit relationship; cares for

tries to kill

Bertha Mason
(Rochester's wife; the crazy woman in the attic)

frightens

Adèle Varens
(Rochester's foreign daughter)

intellectual companions; in love

governess/pupil; companions

St. John, Mary, and Diana Rivers
(Jane's cousins, whom she meets as an adult)

show kindness to

shares fortune with

Mrs. Fairfax
(warmhearted housekeeper of Thornfield)

is kind to

Jane Eyre
(the orphaned protagonist of the story)

despise and are cruel to

The Reeds
(Jane's unpleasant aunt and cousins, who treat her poorly)

spurns

gives fortune to

John Eyre
(Jane's and the Rivers' wealthy uncle who plans to adopt Jane but dies before they ever meet)

is kind to

humiliates

send Jane to his school to be rid of her

Mr. Brocklehurst
(stingy, mean-hearted manager of Lowood School)

Miss Temple
(warmhearted superintendent at Lowood)

CRITICAL COMMENTARIES

Chapter 1

Summary

It is a cold, wet November afternoon when the novel opens at Gateshead, the home of Jane Eyre's relatives, the Reeds. Jane and the Reed children, Eliza, John, and Georgiana sit in the drawing room. Jane's aunt is angry with her, purposely excluding her from the rest of the family, so Jane sits alone in a window seat, reading Bewick's *History of British Birds*.

As she quietly reads, her cousin John torments her, reminding her of her precarious position within the household. As orphaned niece of Mrs. Reed, she should not be allowed to live with gentlemen's children. John throws a book at Jane and she calls him a "murderer" and "slave-driver." The two children fight, and Jane is blamed for the quarrel. As punishment, she is banished to the red-room.

Commentary

Theme

This opening chapter sets up two of the primary themes in the novel: class conflict and gender difference. As a poor orphan living with relatives, Jane feels alienated from the rest of the Reed family, and they certainly do nothing to make her feel more comfortable. John Reed says to Jane: "You have no business to take our books; you are a dependant, mamma says; you have no money; your father left you none; you ought to beg, and not to live here with gentleman's children like us . . . ." John claims the rights of the gentleman, implying that Jane's family was from a lower class. She appears to exist in a no-man's land between the upper and servant classes. By calling John a "murderer," "slave-driver" and "Roman emperor," Jane emphasizes the corruption that is inherent in the ruling classes. Her class difference translates into physical difference, and Jane believes that she is physically inferior to the Reed children.

Jane's argument with John also points to the potential gender conflicts within the text. Not only is Jane at a disadvantage because of her class status, but her position as female leaves her vulnerable to the rules of a patriarchal tyrant. John is an over-indulged only son, described by Jane as "unwholesome" and "thick," someone who habitually gorges himself. Contrasting with Jane's thin, modest appearance, John Reed is a picture of excess: his gluttony feeds his violent emotions, such as constant bullying and punishing of Jane. One of Jane's goals throughout the book will be to create an individual place for herself, free of the tyrannies of her aunt's class superiority and her cousin's gender dominance. By fighting back when John and his mother torment her, Jane refuses the passivity that was expected for a woman in her class position.

Literary Device

Jane's situation as she sits reading Bewick's *History of Birds* provides significant imagery. The red curtains that enclose Jane in her isolated window seat connect with the imagery of the red-room to which Jane is banished at the end of the chapter. The color red is symbolic. Connoting fire and passion, red offers vitality, but also the potential to burn everything that comes in its way to ash. The symbolic energy of the red curtains contrast with the dreary November day that Jane watches outside her window: "a pale blank of mist and cloud." Throughout the book, passion and fire will contrast with paleness and ice. Jane's choice of books is also significant in this scene. Like a bird, she would like the freedom of flying away from the alienation she feels at the Reed's house. The situation of the sea fowl that inhabit "solitary rocks and promontories," is similar to Jane's: Like them, she lives in isolation. The extreme climate of the birds' homes in the Arctic, "that reservoir of frost and snow," the "death-white realms," again creates a contrast with the fire that explodes later in the chapter during John and Jane's violent encounter.

Books provide Jane with an escape from her unhappy domestic situation. For Jane, each picture in Bewick's tale offers a story that sparks her keen imagination. But Jane also says that the book reminds her of the tales that Bessie, one of the Reeds' servants, sometimes tells on winter evenings. Books feed Jane's imagination, offering her a vast world beyond the claustrophobia of Gateshead; they fill her with visions of how rich life could be, rather than how stagnant it actually is. Not a complacent little girl, Jane longs for love and adventure.

Chapters 2 and 3

Summary

As she's being dragged to the red-room, Jane resists her jailors, Bessie and Miss Abbott. After the servants have locked her in, Jane begins observing the red-room. It is the biggest and best room of the mansion, yet is rarely used because Uncle Reed died there.

Looking into a mirror, Jane compares her image to that of a strange fairy. The oddness of being in a death-chamber seems to have stimulated Jane's imagination, and she feels superstitious about her surroundings. She's also contemplative. Why, she wonders, is she always the outcast? The reader learns that Jane's Uncle Reed—her mother's brother—brought her into the household. On his deathbed, he made his wife promise to raise Jane as one of her own children, but obviously, this promise has not been kept.

Suddenly, Jane feels a presence in the room and imagines it might be Mr. Reed, returning to earth to avenge his wife's violation of his last wish. She screams and the servants come running into the room. Jane begs to be removed from the red-room, but neither the servants nor Mrs. Reed have any sympathy for her. Believing that Jane is pretending to be afraid, Mrs. Reed vows that Jane will be freed only if she maintains "perfect stillness and submission." When everyone leaves, Jane faints.

Jane awakens in her own bedroom, surrounded by the sound of muffled voices. She is still frightened but also aware that someone is handling her more tenderly than she has ever been touched before. She feels secure when she recognizes Bessie and Mr. Lloyd, an apothecary, standing near the bed. Bessie is kind to Jane and even tells another servant that she thinks Mrs. Reed was too hard on Jane. Jane spends the next day reading, and Bessie sings her a song.

After a conversation with Jane, Mr. Lloyd recommends that Mrs. Reed send her away to school. Jane is excited about leaving Gateshead and beginning a new life. Overhearing a conversation between Miss Abbot and Bessie, Jane learns that her father was a poor clergyman who married her mother against her family's wishes. As a result, Jane's grandfather Reed disinherited his daughter. A year after their marriage, Jane's father caught typhus while visiting the poor, and both of her parents soon died within a month of each other and left Jane orphaned.

Commentary

Stating that she is resisting her captors like a "rebel slave," Jane continues to use the imagery of oppression begun in the previous chapter. When Miss Abbot admonishes Jane for striking John Reed, Jane's "young master," Jane immediately questions her terminology. Is John really her master; is she his servant? Again, Jane's position within the household is questioned, particularly her class identity. When Mr. Lloyd asks about Jane's relatives on her father's side, Jane replies that she "might have some poor, low relations called Eyre." Mr. Lloyd wonders if Jane would prefer to live with them, and she immediately pictures a world of "ragged clothes, scanty food, fireless grates, rude manners, and debasing vices." Fundamentally, Jane shares the Reed's belief that poor people are morally inferior to the wealthy, and she honestly admits that she isn't "heroic" enough to "purchase liberty at the price of caste." Jane is slowly shaping the parameters of her ideal lifestyle; poverty, she realizes, is not acceptable to her. When Mr. Lloyd suggests school as another option, Jane imagines it as inspiring place, where she could learn to paint, sing, and speak French. Unlike poverty, education offers Jane the possibility of improving her position in society; thus, school may allow her freedom with a potential increase in "caste." Learning about her family background reveals that Jane is not from a "beggarly set," as her aunt had suggested. As a clergyman, her father held an acceptable, even gentlemanly position within Victorian society. Thus, this chapter ends with a refinement in the understanding of Jane's class position.

Miss Abbot, who has the final word on Jane's position, however, calls Jane "a little toad," reminding readers that beauty, as well as class, defines a woman's position within a patriarchal culture. Both Bessie and Miss Abbot believe Jane's plight would be more "moving" if she were as beautiful as her cousin Georgiana who looks "as if she were painted." The novel specifically critiques this "wax-doll" prototype of female beauty, and one of Brontë's goals in this book was to create a poignant, yet *plain*, heroine. As a shy, impoverished, and plain child, Jane decides she is a "useless thing." Thus, she needs to discover her "use," one that is outside the realm of class and beauty.

Color is once again symbolic, revealing the mood of the scene and providing insight into character. While in Chapter 1, Jane was enshrouded by the red curtains, here she is locked within the red-room. Chapter 3 opens with Jane remembering a nightmare image of "a terrible red glare, crossed with thick black bars." For Jane, red has become the color of a hellish nightmare, in which she is jailed behind impenetrable black bars. But this negative connotation soon dissipates, because Jane realizes that the red is simply the glare from her nursery fire. From a sign of evil and hellish fires, red has been transformed into a nurturing, warmth-giving glow. Thus, the significance of symbols and colors in this novel is not static; instead, they change to reflect Jane's emotional and social situation. Skin color is also important. Here the reader learns that John reviles his mother for her "dark skin," a supposedly negative quality that he has inherited from her. The novel appears to support an ethnocentrism that links "darkness" with an unacceptable foreignness, while lightness is affiliated with English purity.

The characterization of Jane is also developed in this chapter. As she gazes at her image in the red-room's mirror, Jane describes herself as a "tiny phantom, half fairy, half imp" from one of Bessie's bedtime stories, a spirit-creature that comes out of "lone, ferny dells in moors" and appears in the eyes of "belated travellers." The association of Jane with a fairy will be repeated throughout the novel, and her notion of appearing, sprite-like, in the eyes of travelers foreshadows her first meeting with Rochester. As fairy, Jane identifies herself as a special, magical creature, and reminds the reader of the importance imagination plays her in her life. Not only is Jane an undefined, almost mythical creature, but the narrative she creates also crosses boundaries by mixing realism and fantasy. We see the first instance of a supernatural intrusion into the novel in this chapter. As Jane sits nervously in the red-room, she imagines a gleam of light shining on the wall and believes it is "a herald of some coming vision from another world." The novel suggests that Jane has psychic powers—she is haunted by other apparitions and by prophetic dreams. Generally, these ghostly visitations prefigure drastic changes in Jane's life, as this one does.

Theme

To improve Jane's spirits, Bessie sings a song that Jane has often delighted in. Now, though, the song suggests only sadness, so Bessie begins another ballad. Like *Gulliver's Travels*, this tune tells the tale of a desolate traveler. The narrator of this song is a "poor orphan child," who has wandered a long way, through wild mountains and dreary twilight. Just as in the previous chapter, Jane meditated upon the purpose of her suffering, the speaker in this song wonders why he or she has been sent "so far and so lonely." The only hope for this lost child is in heaven because God will provide mercy and protection. Implicitly, Bessie suggests that Jane should become a spiritual traveler, looking toward heaven for solace, rather than worrying about her troubles in this world. Jane feels meager comfort in the song's message because she longs to find happiness on earth. Jane's interactions with religious figures and their promise of spiritual salvation will be repeated throughout the text. Should we focus on heaven to the exclusion of earth? In general, Jane doesn't believe humans should be so focused on heaven that they forget the pleasures available for them here on earth.

The narration in this section reminds readers that the tale is being told by an older, wiser Jane remembering her childhood experiences. For example, there are frequent interjections by the older Jane, explaining or apologizing for her feelings. At one point, she says, "Yes, Mrs. Reed, to you I own some fearful pangs of mental suffering. But I ought to forgive you, for your knew not what you did." Jane says she "ought" to forgive Mrs. Reed, but she doesn't necessarily do it. Similarly, this older narrator explains that children are often unable to express their feelings in words; therefore, the reader shouldn't be surprised by the meagerness of Jane's response to Mr. Lloyd's question about the source of her unhappiness in the Reed household. The frequent intrusions of this older voice increase sympathy for Jane, providing more insights on Jane's motivations. Notice that the novel's full title is *Jane Eyre: An Autobiography* and that the title page claims that it was edited, rather than written, by Currer Bell.

Glossary

hummocks small hills.

coney a rabbit.

portent a supernatural warning or hint of danger.

Chapter 4

Summary

Following her discussion with Mr. Lloyd, Jane expects that she will soon be sent away to school. But the only change Jane notices in her status following her experience in the red-room is that the boundary between Jane and the Reed children is more solid. On January 15, after three months of waiting for a change, Jane is finally summoned to the breakfast-room. Here she finds Mr. Brocklehurst waiting for her. Standing like a black pillar, Mr. Brocklehurst interviews Jane about hell, sin, and the Bible. Her aunt's worst suspicions about her moral character are confirmed when Jane declares to Brocklehurst that the "Psalms are not interesting." As a final poke at Jane, Mrs. Reed declares that her niece is a liar, and Brocklehurst promises to alert the other members of the school to Jane's deceitful nature.

Jane resents Mrs. Reed's statements about her character, and when the two are alone together, Jane retaliates against her aunt. Angry and hurt, Jane declares that she is not a liar, that she is glad Mrs. Reed is not her relation, and, finally, that Mrs. Reed is hard-hearted. Jane feels a sense of triumph and exultation, and Mrs. Reed sheepishly leaves the room.

The chapter ends with a conversation between Jane and Bessie. Jane makes Bessie promise to be nice during Jane's final days at Gateshead. Bessie claims she likes Jane more than she likes the Reed children, and confesses that even her mother has noticed how often Jane has been mistreated by the Reeds. In celebration of their new friendship, Bessie tells Jane some of her most enchanting stories and sings her sweetest songs.

Commentary

Mr. Brocklehurst enters the book in this chapter, ushering in the change that will alter Jane's life. On first seeing this grim man, Jane describes him as "a black pillar!—such, at least, appeared to me, at first sight, the straight, narrow, sable-clad shape standing erect on the rug;

the grim face at the top was like a carved mask." A clergyman, Brocklehurst symbolizes Jane's aversion to some of the versions of organized religion. A straight, black, narrow, erect pillar, this man is hard and inflexible in his beliefs, certainly not attributes admired by the adventurous Jane. The "carved mask" of his face suggests his inhumanity, as does Jane's later reference to him as the "stony stranger." Unlike Jane who is associated with fire and energy, this man is cold and aloof as stone, someone with no passion and even less compassion. When Brocklehurst plants her straight in front of him, Jane exclaims, "what a great nose! and what a mouth! and what large, prominent teeth!": Brocklehurst has been transformed into the big bad wolf of fairy-tale fame, waiting to devour the innocent Little Red Riding Hood. From his first introduction into the story, one realizes that this spiritual man will offer Jane little comfort and no salvation.

Besides signaling Jane's lack of interest in the self-righteous religion Brocklehurst professes, their interaction also reminds readers of Jane's general lack of respect for tyrannous authority figures. Her inability to quietly accept unfair treatment becomes pronounced in her interaction with Mrs. Reed. When her aunt tells Brocklehurst that Jane's worst trait is her "deceitful nature," Jane immediately recognizes her lack of power: How can a poor child defend herself from unfair accusations? When Brocklehurst leaves, Jane is filled with a "passion of resentment," contrasting clearly with Mrs. Reed's "eye of ice" that dwells "freezingly" on Jane. Indeed, Mrs. Reed's iciness incites Jane's passions, causing her entire body to shake, "thrilled with ungovernable excitement" and her mind has become a "ridge of lighted heath, alive, glancing, devouring." Following an outburst against her aunt, Jane feels a sensation of freedom and triumph. In fact, she declares herself the "winner of the field" and revels in her "conqueror's solitude." Has she simply stepped into her cousin John's role, becoming for a moment the "Roman emperor" she had earlier critiqued him for being?

Struck by the fate of Jane's enemies, many critics have viewed this novel as Jane's revenge fantasy. As the story progresses, notice what happens to Jane's attackers; all seem to meet with misfortune and unhappiness. Jane's fiery, passionate nature transforms as the novel progresses, and she learns to balance passion and reason. In this scene, Jane's passion quickly drains away, and she's left with its aftertaste, "metallic and corroding," showing her that excessive emotions will not lead to happiness. Yet releasing her inner fire has a positive result: Because of it she befriends Bessie at the end of the chapter. This conversation reveals Bessie's sympathy—even affection—for Jane.

Chapter 5

Summary

January 19, the date of Jane's departure from Gateshead has arrived. She rises at five o'clock in the morning, so that she'll be ready for the six o'clock coach. None of the family rises to bid Jane farewell, and she happily journeys far away from the Reeds. The porter's wife is surprised that Mrs. Reed is allowing such a young child to travel alone. Jane's imaginative nature is once again apparent, and she worries that kidnappers will snatch her away at the inn where the coach stops for dinner.

The day of Jane's arrival at Lowood is rainy, windy, and dark. Jane is led through the unfamiliar, labyrinthine halls of Lowood, until she reaches a large room in which eighty other girls sit doing their homework. Soon it is bedtime, and Jane wearily makes her way to bed. The next day, Jane follows the full routine of the school, studying from predawn until five o'clock in the evening. The chapter is filled with Jane's observations of the school. Jane discovers the kind Miss Temple and the unreasonable Miss Scatcherd, who unfairly punishes Helen Burns. While solitary and isolated through most of the day, Jane does converse with Helen, who tells Jane that Lowood is a charity institution for orphan children. She also learns that Miss Temple must answer to Mr. Brocklehurst in all she does.

Commentary

Jane is making progress in her journey of self-knowledge, and has now progressed from Gateshead (note the significance of the name, as the starting point of Jane's quest) to Lowood. Its name alerts the reader that the school will be a "low" place for Jane, and, thus, it appears on her first day. Modeled after the Clergy Daughters School at Cowan Bridge where Charlotte Brontë and her sisters Maria, Elizabeth, and Emily were sent, Lowood is not appealing. The school day begins before dawn, the students are offered meager rations of burnt and unappetizing food, and the grounds surrounding the school are blighted and decayed. The chapter shows the harsh realities of charity-school life in Victorian times.

Besides acquainting us with the rigors of Lowood, the chapter also introduces us to two women who will have significant impact on Jane's development: Miss Temple and Helen Burns. Miss Temple's name signifies Jane's worshipful feeling for Lowood's superintendent, as does her appearance: she is tall, fair, and shapely, with a "benignant light" in her eyes and a "stately" posture. Notice how Miss Temple's appearance contrasts with the stony, dark, rigid exterior of her employer, Mr. Brocklehurst. Supplying the compassion he lacks, Miss Temple orders a decent lunch for her students to compensate for their burnt breakfast.

Another hero in Jane's story, Helen Burns, is introduced in this chapter. What does Helen Burns' name signify? She is burning with a passion for heaven, and her fate is to die of a fever. Burns is based on Charlotte Brontë's oldest sister, Maria, who died when she was twelve years old after contracting consumption at the Clergy Daughters School. Brontë's second-oldest sister, Elizabeth, also died from this disease, caught at the unsanitary and damp school. Both Charlotte and Emily were withdrawn from the school before the following winter for the sake of their health. Like Helen Burns, Maria was known for the precocity of her thinking; Mr. Brontë said that "he could converse with her [Maria] on any of the leading topics of the day with as much freedom and pleasures as with any grown-up person."

When Jane first notices Helen, her friend is reading Samuel Johnson's didactic tome, *Rasselas*, an essay arguing that happiness is often unobtainable. Although she enjoys reading, Jane isn't interested in Helen's book because it doesn't contain any fairies or genii. Like Jane, Helen is a poor, lonely child, but her method of dealing with her problems contrasts with Jane's, as is apparent in the interaction with Miss Scatcherd. After being unfairly disciplined by Miss Scatcherd, Helen neither cries nor looks humiliated; instead, she accepts her situation with composure and grace. Wondering how Helen can accept this treatment so quietly and firmly, Jane notices that Helen seems to be "thinking of something beyond her punishment," and her sight seems to have "gone down into her heart," emphasizing Helen's focus on spiritual rather than material matters. Jane is fascinated with Helen's self-possession, which signals a depth of character that is new to her. At this point in the story, Jane doesn't know how to judge Helen: Is she good or bad? Jane's goals in this first section of the book to learn to recognize character and to find a role model.

Chapters 6 and 7

Summary

When the girls wake for breakfast on Jane's second morning at Lowood, they discover that the water in the pitchers is frozen. Before, she had been merely a spectator at Lowood, but now Jane will become an actor, participating fully in the events at the school. As Jane sits sewing, she notices once again how unfairly Helen Burns is treated: Miss Scatcherd picks on Helen for inconsequential things, such as poking her chin unpleasantly or not holding her head up. Despite Miss Scatcherd's criticisms, Helen appears to be one of the brightest students in the class. She has answers for the most difficult questions.

Later in the evening, Jane converses once again with Helen. She learns more about Helen's philosophy of life and her doctrine of endurance. Helen praises Jane for her virtues, such as the ability to pay careful attention during lessons. In contrast, Helen believes she herself suffers from carelessness and poor concentration, spending too much time daydreaming about her home in Deepden, Northumberland. While Jane thinks Helen should fight against injustice, Helen tells her to follow Christ's example by loving her enemies.

Jane's first quarter at Lowood passes, and Chapter 7 records Jane's general impressions of her first three months at the school. Again, she focuses on the harshness of life at Lowood: the severe cold, near starvation, and the long hours spent memorizing the Church Catechism and listening to long sermons. Fortunately for Jane, Mr. Brocklehurst, the financial manager of Lowood, is absent during most of this time. Finally, he appears at the school. Jane is worried at his arrival, because she remembers Mrs. Reed's comments to him about Jane's deceitfulness and Mr. Brocklehurst's promise to warn the teachers at the school of Jane's unsavory character.

During his visit, Jane accidentally drops her slate. Brocklehurst immediately brands her as careless. Although Miss Temple tells her not to be afraid of punishment, Jane is soon made the dunce of the school. Brocklehurst stands her on a stool and announces to the entire school that Jane is a liar. No one is to speak to Jane for the rest of the day, but Helen silently supports her friend by smiling every time she passes Jane's stool.

Commentary

The significant differences between Jane's and Helen's philosophies of life become apparent in this chapter. While Jane is always ready to fight against her enemies, Helen practices a doctrine of patient endurance. Although Helen accepts all punishment without a tear, the "spectacle" of her friend's suffering causes Jane to quiver with "unavailing and impotent anger." What are the reasons for Helen's endurance? First, she doesn't want to be a burden on her family, causing them grief by misbehaving. She also feels all people are required to bear what fate has ordained for them. Her belief in predestination, the idea that one's life is guided by fate rather than choice, shows her adherence to the philosophy of *Calvinism*. Founded by the Swiss theologian John Calvin, a leader in the Protestant Reformation movement, Calvinists follow a strict moral code and believe in the salvation of a select few who have been elected by God's grace.

Although Jane thinks Helen may have access to some deep spiritual truth, Jane cannot understand Helen's "doctrine of endurance" or her sympathy for her torturer. Unlike Helen, Jane believes in being good to people who are good to her. When struck without reason, the victim needs to "strike back again very hard," in order to teach the assailant a lesson. As readers saw in her final conversation with Aunt Reed, Jane firmly believes in retaliation and vengeance. Helen argues that a true Christian should mimic Jesus by loving, blessing, and benefiting her neighbors. In Helen's opinion, Jane should even try to forgive her Aunt Reed, because life is too short for "nursing animosity." With her mind aimed squarely at heaven, Helen urges Jane to remember the eternal spirit that animates her temporary, corruptible body. Helen offers a view of Christianity that contrasts with the strict, hypocritical religion of Mr. Brocklehurst. While her compassion for other people is admirable and her rejection of vengeance and retaliation temper Jane's passionate anger, Helen will not offer Jane a completely acceptable model of Christianity because of her refusal to live in the real world. She is too much like the poor orphan in Bessie's song who rejected the real world in her dreams of heaven.

Brocklehurst's hypocrisy is highlighted in this chapter. At the arrival of this dour man, who looks "longer, narrower, and more rigid than ever," Jane is immediately upset. Her intuitive dislike for him is clearly justified in this scene. Brocklehurst insists that the girls eat a starvation-level diet so that they don't become accustomed to "habits of luxury and indulgence." Brocklehurst justifies this extreme lifestyle by referring to Christian doctrines. Like the primitive Christians and tormented martyrs, the girls should revel in their suffering and accept Jesus' consolations. Brocklehurst's hypocrisy becomes most apparent when his own wife and daughters enter the classroom. As Brocklehurst lectures Miss Temple on the need to cut off the girls' long hair—it's a sign of vanity—his wife and daughters walk into the room, ornately dressed in velvet, silk, and furs. Jane notes that his daughters' hair is "elaborately curled" and that his wife wears fake French curls.

Character Insight

Rather than arguing with Brocklehurst, as the headstrong Jane might have, Miss Temple attempts to hide her emotions, but Jane notices that her face appears to become as cold and fixed as marble, "especially her mouth, closed as if it would have required a sculptor's chisel to open it." Miss Temple turns to stone rather than confront her boss. While her compassion, elegance, and reverence for learning make her a valuable role model for Jane, Miss Temple's failure to confront injustice directly is unacceptable to Jane.

Calling Jane an "interloper and an alien," Brocklehurst attempts to place Jane back into the inferior, outsider position she occupied at Gateshead. Although she is initially humiliated by his punishment, feeling that she is standing on a "pedestal of infamy," Helen offers solace. The light that shines in Helen's eyes when she walks past Jane's stool sends an "extraordinary sensation" through Jane, as if a "hero" has walked past a "slave or victim, and imparted strength in the transit." Again, Jane employs the language of heroism and slavery—but while she had been a "rebel slave" at the Reeds, here Helen's heroism passes into Jane so that she can relinquish her victimization. Again Helen's power is spiritual rather than corporeal: Her eyes are inspired by a "strange light" and her smile is angelic. Through Helen's actions, Jane learns that heroism isn't achieved by vengeance, but by dignity, intelligence, and courage. Equally, she learns to change her behavior by changing her attitude; Helen's mere smile turns Jane's shame into strength.

Chapter 8

Summary

At five o'clock, school is dismissed for tea. The spell she has been under dissolves and Jane collapses on the floor in grief. She feels all of her successes at Lowood have now been destroyed by Brocklehurst's unfair accusations. Jane wonders how Helen can be friends with a girl that the world has branded a liar. Helen tells Jane she is exaggerating: Only eighty people of the hundreds of millions in the world heard Brocklehurst, and most of those people probably pity, rather than dislike Jane.

Miss Temple also befriends Jane, allowing her to present her side of the story. Miss Temple promises to write to Mr. Lloyd for verification of Jane's statements; if his reply agrees with Jane's, she will be publicly cleared. For Miss Temple, though, Jane is already clear. Jane and Helen share a sumptuous tea with their teacher; indeed, Jane declares the seed-cake Miss Temple offers is like "ambrosia." Miss Temple then turns her attention to Helen, and the two begin a conversation about French and Latin authors. Jane is amazed by the extent of Helen's knowledge.

Mr. Lloyd replies to Miss Temple's letter, corroborating Jane's statements, so Miss Temple assembles the entire school and vindicates Jane from all of the charges Brocklehurst had leveled against her. With this load off her mind, Jane returns diligently to work, quickly rising to a higher class. Soon she is learning French and drawing, and happier at Lowood than she ever was at Gateshead.

Commentary

While Jane, Miss Temple, and Helen Burns become closer friends in this chapter, the differences in their personalities also become more obvious. Helen, for example, is not afraid of solitude; therefore, she believes that even if all the world hated her, but she approved of herself, she would not be without friends. For Jane, this is not true; she declares, "if others don't love me, I would rather die than live—I cannot bear to be solitary and hated." The promise of love and glory in a distant heaven does not appease Jane; she also requires human warmth and affections during her time on earth. When Helen declares that Jane thinks too much of the love of human beings and too little of the "kingdom of spirits," Jane recognizes an implicit sadness in Helen's statements. In some sense, Helen's longing for the afterlife reveals an obsession with death. Helen coughs after speaking, foreshadowing her early death, but also providing insight on her focus on heaven: Believing she will die young, Helen is preparing herself by romanticizing the afterworld.

Again, Jane's description of Helen emphasizes her spiritual nature. For example, the beauty in her eyes is not attributed to their color or long eyelashes, but to meaning and radiance; "her soul sat on her lips, and language flowed . . . [with] pure, full, fervid eloquence." Indeed, the sophistication of Helen's understanding of life and literature are astonishing for a fourteen-year-old. Perhaps, Jane thinks, knowledge of her impending death is leading her to live within a brief span as much as many people live in a longer life; like a candle in the wind, Helen burns brightly. Through her relationship with Helen, Jane learns to look beyond appearance and discover people's inner nature.

Miss Temple's moderate language, together with Helen's instructions against the overindulgence of anger, are evidently altering Jane's character. Rejecting "gall and wormwood," Jane tells Miss Temple a moderate version of her life with the Reeds and believes that "[t]hus restrained and simplified, it sounded more credible." Through Helen's instruction, and Miss Temple's example, Jane is learning to tell a realistic and reasonable narrative, lessons that have probably fed into her autobiography. Hysteria and raw emotion don't reveal the truth as effectively as a subdued, but honest tale. But Jane will never fully achieve the moderation of either of her friends. Upon seeing the pasteboard with the word "slattern" hanging around Helen's neck, Jane, her soul burning in her body, rips is off and throws it into the fire. Perhaps resignation is not always appropriate. Even if Miss Temple's and Helen's mild tempers never rub off completely on Jane, their impressive knowledge of literature inspires her quest for education. One day, she will create an ideal life, one that combines Miss Temple's refinement and Helen's spirituality with a spark of Jane's passion.

Chapter 9

Summary

Spring arrives at Lowood, and the privations lessen. With new growth comes hope. Jane finds beauty in the natural world surrounding Lowood, a beauty that had been masked by winter's frosts. But within this pleasure, there is also pain. The forest dell that nurtures the school, the "low wood," also brings a pestilence bred by dampness—typhus. Combined with semi-starvation and neglected colds, the dampness causes forty-five of the eighty students to fall ill with this dangerous disease. The few who are well, including Jane, are allowed to play outside without supervision. Jane notes the contrast between the death within the school and the beauty of May outside its doors.

While Jane is enjoying nature's beauty with her new friend, Mary Ann Wilson, Helen Burns is slowly dying, not of typhus, but of consumption. Jane doesn't realize the seriousness of this disease until she learns from the nurse that Helen will soon die. Jane feels she must embrace Helen one last time before she dies and sneaks into Miss Temple's room, where Helen has been staying during her illness. During the two friends' final conversation, Helen insists she is happy, because she will escape great suffering by dying young. Helen dies in Jane's arms, while the two girls sleep. Fifteen years later, Jane marks Helen's grave with a gray marble tablet labeled "*Resurgam.*"

Commentary

Like the previous few chapters, this one emphasizes the contrast between the spiritual and material worlds through the characters of Helen and Jane. The chapter opens with the brilliance of spring: The world becomes green and fertile, bursting with "wild primrose plants." While Jane and her new friend, Mary Ann Wilson, happily enjoy this luxurious natural world, Lowood School has become marked with pestilence: Typhus is quickly killing half the girls in the school. Jane vividly contrasts life and death, showing Lowood as the begetter both of May's brilliance and of typhus' deadliness. Pain and pleasure are necessarily twinned.

While Jane is innocently reveling in nature, her friend Helen Burns lies dying of consumption. Jane hasn't forgotten her old friend in her new pleasures. After spending a beautiful day outdoors, Jane suddenly imagines, for the first time, how sad lying on a sickbed would be, how awful to be in danger of dying; Jane finds the mundane world pleasant and isn't ready yet to die. This revelation leads her to recognize that the present is the only moment we have: Both the past and the future are "formless cloud and vacant depth." Following this revelation, Jane learns of Helen's imminent death, and her meditations provide her with understanding of what death means; for Jane, it means "tottering, and plunging amid that chaos." But death has a very different meaning for Helen.

The final conversation between the two girls emphasizes their different understanding of the world. While Jane finds pleasure and beauty in the natural world, Helen longs for the release of heaven. Helen assures Jane that her mind is peaceful, but her final words also contain a hint of sadness. Here we learn, for example, that Helen has no family to mourn her, because her father has recently married and will not miss her. Helen feels that an early death will save her from great suffering. Because she has no father in the earthly world to mourn her, Helen looks to God, the "mighty universal Parent" to comfort her. Jane, on the other hand, wonders, "Where is God? What is God?" Uncertain of spiritual salvation, Jane comforts her friend in the best way she can: by hugging her tight, providing corporeal comfort. Despite her courage, Helen seems to find comfort in Jane's arms, asking her friend to remain with her while she sleeps. The chapter gives insight into Helen's spiritual nature: She rejects an earthly world that offers her little love and few chances for a better future. While Helen's resignation allows her to die with dignity, Jane's courage leads her to face life with zest. The chapter emphasizes Jane's inability to put her faith completely in either God or his heaven. For Jane, heaven exists here on earth, in the beauties of a May day.

Glossary

Resurgam I will rise again.

Chapter 10

Summary

Eight years pass before Jane again picks up her narrative. Following an investigation into the cause of the typhus epidemic at Lowood, Mr. Brocklehurst is publicly humiliated, and a new building is erected. Brocklehurst remains the treasurer for the school, but other, more enlightened, gentlemen become the school's inspectors and it becomes a "truly useful and noble institution." Jane remains at Lowood for eight years: six as a student and two as a teacher.

Jane enjoys excelling in her studies, but after two years as a teacher, Jane needs a change. First, Miss Temple marries and moves far away, taking with her Jane's "serene" feelings about Lowood. Jane's old need for adventure returns and she longs to experience the perils of the real world. Since arriving at the school, Jane has never quitted it, even for holidays, and she now dreams of "liberty" and a "new servitude." Jane places an ad in the newspaper for a job as a governess. A response arrives from a Mrs. Fairfax of Thornfield, Millcote, who needs a governess for a little girl, and Jane decides to take the job. Before leaving for her new position, Jane has an unexpected visit from Bessie Lee, the Reeds' nurse-maid. From her, she learns that none of the Reed children has turned out well: Georgiana tried to elope with a young man and Eliza jealously tattled on them, and John leads a life of excess. Bessie is impressed with Jane's ladylike appearance and accomplishments. Jane also learns that her father's brother, John Eyre had come to the Reeds seeking Jane seven years ago. Unfortunately, he couldn't visit her at Lowood, because he was leaving for Madeira to make his fortune.

Commentary

Another portion of Jane's journey is about to end, and its demise is signaled by Miss Temple's departure from Lowood. Over time, Miss Temple has become more than a teacher to Jane: she is also mother, governess, and companion. Miss Temple's guidance has tempered Jane's impulsiveness and fire so that her thoughts have become "harmonious," her feelings "regulated," and her appearance "disciplined and subdued."

But this appearance is only that: an external shell. When Miss Temple leaves Lowood, the shell cracks and Jane realizes that many of her new feelings didn't reflect her true nature, but were merely "borrowings" from her teacher. Jane's nature yearns for sensation, excitement, and the knowledge gained through experience, rather than the peaceful isolation of Lowood. The landscape reflects Jane's thoughts: She would like to leave Lowood's safe garden and explore the remote blue peaks in the distance.

Literary Device

As Jane's departure from Gateshead was signaled by her pseudo-supernatural experience in the red-room, her movement away from Lowood also has a paranormal component. Meditating upon the best means for discovering "a new servitude," Jane is visited by a "kind fairy," who offers her a solution. This psychic counselor gives Jane very specific advice: Place an advertisement in the local newspaper, with answers addressed to J.E.—and do it immediately. The fairy's plan works, and Jane soon has a new employment opportunity.

Jane is happy to see that the handwriting in the letter is old-fashioned, like that of an elderly lady. Why? Because it is important for her, as a single woman in Victorian culture, to maintain her decorum; "above all things, I wished the result of my endeavours to be respectable, proper, *en règle*." The chapter's emphasis on propriety and decency is continued during Bessie's conversation with Jane. In fact, the novel continues to ask what it means to be a "lady" or a "gentleman." Bessie is impressed because Jane has become "quite a lady": She can now play the piano, draw and speak French better than the Miss Reeds, yet they are still considered her social superiors, as is their alcoholic brother, John. Jane's social status may be higher, however, than the Reeds think. According to Bessie, Jane's uncle, who stopped at the Reeds' home on his search for Jane, "looked quite a gentleman." The conversation emphasizes the ambiguities of Jane's family's class status and of the class system in general. Should a lady be judged on her academic accomplishments, money, or family name? This question will become more pronounced as the novel progresses.

Glossary

en règle in order.

Chapter 11

Summary

Jane sits waiting at the George Inn at Millcote, because no one has arrived from Thornfield to pick her up. Just as Jane is becoming anxious, a servant arrives for her. Despite its imposing architecture, Thornfield is inviting. Mrs. Fairfax proves to be a neat, mild-looking elderly lady, who greets Jane kindly. Surprised, Jane finds herself to be the object of more attention than she has ever before received.

For the first time, Jane learns of the existence of Mr. Rochester, the owner of Thornfield. Jane also discovers that her new pupil, Adèle Varens, is Rochester's ward. Meeting eight-year-old Adèle, Jane is surprised to find she and her nurse, Sophie, are French and speak little English. Adèle's mother was a dancer and singer, and Adèle is also an adept performer, who sings an opera song for Jane. After her mother was taken to the "Holy Virgin," Adèle lived with a Madame Frédéric and her husband for a while, but the Frédérics were too poor to look after her, so Rochester kindly brought her to England.

Mrs. Fairfax gives Jane some information about Rochester and his family: He is somewhat "peculiar," but a good master, and in general, the Rochesters have been a "violent" rather than a "quiet" family. As she tours the house with Mrs. Fairfax, Jane suddenly hears a strange, disquieting laugh. Mrs. Fairfax tells her that the laugh belongs to Grace Poole, an eccentric servant.

Commentary

A new stage of Jane's life has begun, and she feels it will be a good one. From the simplicity and peacefulness of Lowood, Jane has entered the stately, upper-class realm of Thornfield. The chapter begins with a direct address from the narrator, who tells readers that each new chapter in a novel is like a new scene in a play; when she draws the curtain, readers must imagine themselves in a new place. Thus, she draws the reader into her performance; not a passive reader, but one actively involved in imagining the people and places the novel describes. In addressing the reader directly, the narrator identifies her reader as companion and friend, someone who is expected to peer into Jane's life and vicariously share her experiences.

Class issues are addressed once again. As an upper-servant, Mrs. Fairfax feels a great difference between herself and the other servants in the house. For example, she likes Leah and John, "but then you see they are only servants, and one can't converse with them on terms of equality; one must keep them at due distance for fear of losing one's authority." The strict hierarchical system in England requires that everyone maintain their proper place, yet, as the novel shows, the differences between classes are constantly blurred. As a governess, Jane will be in the same category as Mrs. Fairfax: neither a member of the family nor a member of the serving class.

The British tried to maintain hierarchies not only between different social classes, but also between themselves and foreigners. As a French citizen, Adèle is, therefore, an exotic. While Jane emphasizes that her own clothes are extremely simple, and her entire appearance "Quaker-like," Adèle's style is more extravagant. Her excess is apparent in the operatic song she chooses, the tale of a woman whose lover has forsaken her. The song's subject, which Jane feels is in very bad taste for a child, hints at Adèle's mother's sexuality, but also shows that Adèle herself will need to be tamed to meet proper British moral standards. This will be Jane's goal, along with geography, history, and English lessons.

Glossary

bonne a nurse.

C'est là ma gouvernante? Is this my governess?

Mais oui, certainment. Yes, certainly.

La Ligue des Rats: fable de La Fontaine "The Plot of the Rats": a fable by Jean de la Fontaine.

Qu'avez-vous donc? lui dit un de ces rats; parlez! "What do you have, then?" says one of the rats, "Speak!"

Mesdames, vous êtes servies! J'ai bien faim, moi! Ladies, you are served! I am very hungry.

Chapter 12

Summary

Thornfield meets up to Jane's initial expectations: calm and comfortable. Adèle is a lively, spoiled child, but she is also obedient and teachable. Jane still longs for the busy world of the city, for variety, for conversation with her peers. A restlessness exists in Jane's nature that causes her pain. Walking along the corridor of the third story of the house is her only way of easing this discomfort.

Several months pass, and one day in January, Jane takes a long walk through the fields surrounding Thornfield. As she sits on a hill, watching the moon rising, a noise breaks her reverie; a horse is coming up the lane. While Jane watches for the horse, she thinks of a North-of-England spirit Bessie had once told her about, called a Gytrash. Assuming the form of a horse, mule or large dog, the *Gytrash* often scared lonely travelers. After thinking this, Jane sees a huge Newfoundland dog gliding through the bushes. A man rides into view, and breaking Jane's spell. His horse slips on a patch of ice, and the man falls. Jane tells the man, who is in his late-thirties and not handsome, that she is the governess at Thornfield and helps him hobble to his horse. Then horse, man, and dog all vanish. Meditating upon the experience, Jane is happy to have offered active assistance. She returns to Thornfield and learns that the man she helped was her employer—Mr. Rochester.

Commentary

In this chapter the reader is shown another example of Jane's restlessness. The quiet haven of Thornfield has become stagnant and lonely, and the uniform, still life it offers provides "an existence whose very privilege of security and ease" that Jane is becoming unable to appreciate. Yearning for a life of excitement, variety, and intellectual stimulation, Jane isn't satisfied with the monotony of Mrs. Fairfax or the youthful simplicity of Adèle. In consequence, Jane spends much time within her own imagination, opening her inward ear to "a tale my imagination created, and narrated continuously; quickened with all incident, life, fire, feeling, that I desired and had not in my actual existence." Jane suggests that her problems are gender-related. Women need active pursuits, just as men do; they, too, need to stretch their intellectual limits. Like men, they suffer from rigid restraint and absolute stagnation. Indeed, Jane believes men are "narrow-minded" to suggest women should satisfy themselves with domestic pursuits. Arguing that a silent rebellion is brewing in women's minds, the novel's message is revolutionary.

Literary Device

Jane's momentous meeting with Rochester is significant at many levels. First, her association of Rochester's horse and dog with the mythical Gytrash brings another supernatural element into the story. The massive dog is "a lion-like creature with long hair and a huge head" (at the end of the novel, Rochester will also be described as lionish) Jane is almost surprised when it doesn't look up to her "with strange preter-canine eyes." In English folklore, the Gytrash often appears to warn people of the coming death of a friend or relative, but it also adds a mythic feeling to Jane and Rochester's first meeting that makes their later relationship seem more extraordinary. It is also significant that Rochester is disabled during their first meeting. Having fallen from his horse, Rochester requires Jane's assistance. Many critics have argued that this incident helps to establish equality between the two characters. It also foreshadows Rochester's dependence upon Jane at the end of the novel. Jane also limits Rochester's powers by emphasizing that he is neither handsome nor heroic-looking. Finally, Rochester recognizes Jane's ambiguous class and social position through his inability to guess her role in the Thornfield household; he realizes she isn't a servant, yet her clothes aren't fine enough for a lady's-maid. On Jane's part, she is happy to have left behind, even for a moment, her passive, dependent, feminine status by offering active, and necessary assistance.

Glossary

par parenthèse by the way.

Revenez bientôt, ma bonne amie, ma chère Mdlle Jeanette. Hurry back, my good friend, my dear Miss Jane.

Chapter 13

Summary

Life at Thornfield changes following Rochester's arrival. Jane and Adèle are forced to abandon the library because Rochester needs to use it as a meeting room. Before, silence had ruled; now, the house it filled with new voices. Jane likes the place better now that it has a master. Adèle finds it impossible to concentrate on her lessons because she's so busy wondering what presents Rochester has brought for her.

Jane isn't pleased with the "additional ceremony" of dressing up for tea with Rochester. Jane again notes the firm, decisiveness of his face, which is imposing rather than beautiful. Rochester's stiff, impatient formality with Jane intrigues her more than "finished politeness" would have. Questioning her about her family and discovering that her parents are dead, Rochester concludes that Jane is a fairy. He then judges her accomplishments, her piano playing and drawing. While he finds her playing average, Rochester is impressed by Jane's drawings. At nine o'clock, Rochester dismisses the women.

Mrs. Fairfax tells Jane more of Edward Rochester's history. His father, Old Mr. Rochester, and brother, Rowland, plotted against him, so Edward was forced into a painful position, of which Mrs. Fairfax knows nothing. Edward broke away from the family, only returning to Thornfield nine years ago when his brother died and he thus inherited the property.

Commentary

The relationship between Jane and Rochester develops in this chapter. Rochester is a grim and unfriendly man, but Jane enjoys his gruffness, because she wouldn't have known how to respond to grace, elegance, or politeness. Because Rochester is so natural, not acting a part, Jane feels she can also be open and honest during her interactions with him. Continuing with the mythic, almost supernatural theme of their initial encounter, Rochester reveals that he thought Jane was a fairy who had bewitched his horse when they first met. Rochester repeatedly refers to Jane as a sprite or elfin character, claiming that the "men in green" are her relatives, repeating the associations between Jane and fairies that began early in the novel, and emphasizing the mystical aspects of her personality. As an orphan, Jane's past and future are both open; she is not required to cater to anyone else's desires for her; if she wants to claim fairies for kin, she can. Significantly, both Jane and Rochester give their initial meeting a fairy-tale significance, suggesting their relationship will be ideal or special in some way.

After gazing at her drawings, Rochester finds that they, too, are "elfish." Jane confides to her readers that her "spiritual eye" provided her with the images for the drawing, which are only "a pale portrait of the thing I had conceived." Jane's daydreaming has been channeled into her artistic productions, so that her passion and restlessness have a creative outlet. As Rochester notes, the drawings are not typical schoolgirl productions, but have strange, sometimes violent subjects: a drowned corpse; a vision of the Evening Star with dark and wild eyes; and a colossal head resting upon an iceberg. Rochester immediately wonders if Jane was happy when she created these images, and she replies that to paint them was "to enjoy one of the keenest pleasures I have ever know." For her, happiness comes through artistic creation, and the starkness and beauty of the pictures signals the depth of her character. Despite her pleasure in creative work, Jane is upset by the contrast between her ideas and the actual pictures. Is this also true of the autobiography? Is this also an artistic product that doesn't fulfill the artist's desires? Still, Rochester is impressed by the glimpses the drawings give of Jane's inner visions. As "elfish" productions, they have spiritual and magical power over him.

Glossary

ami a friend.

Et cela doit . . . n'est-ce pas, mademoiselle? And this must mean there's a present inside for me, and perhaps for you also, miss. Mr. Rochester asked about you: He wanted to know the name of my governess, and if she was petite, rather thin, and a bit pale. I said yes: because it's true, isn't it, miss?

N'est-ce pas . . . petite coffre? Sir, isn't there a present for Miss Eyre in your little trunk?

Chapters 14 and 15

Summary

At first, Jane sees little of Rochester. During their brief encounters, she notices his moodiness, but it doesn't upset her. Finally, one evening, he summons Adèle and Jane, offering Adèle her long-awaited present. Jane notices that Rochester is in a friendlier mood than usual, probably due to his dinner wine. Rochester enjoys Jane's frank, sincere manner, and confesses that he hasn't lived the purest, most innocent life. They discuss sin, remorse, and reformation. Finding Jane a good listener, Rochester speaks to her as freely as if he were writing his thoughts in a diary. He says he has given up his shameful lifestyle, and is ready to begin a new, pure life. Rochester tells Jane he is rearing Adèle in order to expiate the sins of his youth.

In Chapter 15, Rochester tells Jane about his passion for Céline Varens, a French opera-dancer whom he naively believed loved him. One night, however, Céline arrived home with another man and they mocked Rochester's "deformities"; Rochester overheard the conversation and immediately ended the relationship. Céline told Rochester that Adèle was his daughter, but he isn't sure because she doesn't look anything like him. Several years later, Céline abandoned her daughter and ran away to Italy with a musician. Although he refuses to recognize Adèle as his daughter, Rochester took pity on the abandoned and destitute child and brought her to England.

At two o'clock one morning, Jane hears a demoniac laugh outside of her bedroom door and the sound of fingers brushing against the panels. She thinks it might be Pilot, Rochester's dog, wandering the hallways, but then she hears a door opening. Going into the hallway, she sees smoke billowing from Rochester's room. She rushes into his chamber and discovers the curtains on fire and his bed surrounded by tongues of flame. Unable to wake him, she deluges the bed with water. Rochester won't let Jane call for help; instead, he says that he must pay a visit to the third floor. He tells Jane that Grace Poole was the culprit and then thanks her warmly for saving his life. He asks Jane to keep the incident a secret.

Commentary

Early critics of the novel, such as Elizabeth Rigby, objected to Rochester's character, finding him "coarse and brutal." In her opinion, the novel as a whole showed an unwholesome "coarseness of language and laxity of tone." The conversation between Jane and Rochester in these chapters was shocking to a Victorian audience; as Rochester himself admits, telling the story of his affair with an opera-dancer to an inexperienced girl seems odd. He justifies his action by arguing that Jane's strong character is not likely to "take infection" from this tale of immorality; indeed, he claims that he cannot "blight" Jane, but she might "refresh" him. Again, Rochester hopes that his relationship with Jane will bring innocence and freshness back into his life.

Just as women need to lead active lives, Brontë argues, they should not be sheltered from life's seamier side. Not only does the Rochester's past reveal his growing faith in Jane, it also shows the Byronic side of his nature. Like Lord Byron, a romantic, passionate, and cynical poet of the early nineteenth century, Rochester let himself be ruled by his "grande passion" for Céline, despite its immorality. Rochester is not afraid to flout social conventions. This is also apparent in his developing relationship with Jane; rather than maintaining the proper class boundaries, Rochester makes Jane feel "as if he were my relation rather than my master."

Rochester's responses to Adèle provide insights on his past life, which help identity the reasons for his attraction to Jane. Adèle Varens provides Rochester with a daily reminder of his past indiscretions. Attracted to luxury, to satin robes and silk stockings, Adèle displays a materialism Rochester dislikes primarily because it reminds him of her mother, Céline Varens, who charmed the "English gold" out of his "British breeches." Emphasizing his British innocence, Rochester's comments are ethnocentric, but they also show that he dislikes the "artificiality" and the materialism of women who, like Céline, are pleased with "nothing but gold dust."

Rochester continues to create a contrast between Céline's superficiality and Jane's sincerity. While Céline pretended to admire his physical appearance, for example, Jane honestly tells him that she doesn't find him handsome. Céline presents an unsavory model of femininity, but also an image of unattractive foreignness. Jane's comment implies that the English, unlike their French neighbors, are deep, rather than superficial, spiritual rather than materialistic. Not only does the novel question class and gender roles, but it also develops a specific ideal of Britishness. Jane provides a prototype of the proper English woman, who is frank, sincere, and lacking in personal vanity. Rochester is intrigued by the honesty of Jane's conversation and the spirituality of her drawings, which clearly contrast with the values of the women with whom he has previously consorted. Honestly admitting that his life hasn't been admirable, Rochester is now looking for happiness, for "sweet, fresh pleasure." Rochester's goal is self-transformation, a reformation to be enacted through his relationships with women.

Literary Device

The end of Chapter 15 takes a strange, almost supernatural turn. Beginning with Rochester's revelation of his illicit passion for Céline Varens, the chapter, not insignificantly, ends with an image of "tongues of flame" darting around his bed. Rochester's sexual indiscretions have become literalized in the vision of his burning bed, an excess that Jane douses. The scene foreshadows Jane's role in channeling Rochester's sexual profligacy into a properly domestic, reproductive passion. Jane's final dream also foreshadows the direction of her relationship with Rochester: She is "tossed on a buoyant but unquiet sea, where billows of trouble rolled under surges of joy." Unable to reach the "sweet hills" that await her, Jane must remain for awhile in the unquiet sea. Recognizing her growing love for Rochester, Jane's unconscious warns her that their relationship will be a rocky one. Rather than letting herself be blown around by the chaos of passion and delirium, she should maintain her sense and judgment. In this novel, the bounds of reality continually expand, so that dreams and visions have as much validity as reason.

Glossary

Rencontre a meeting.

petit coffre a small trunk.

Ma boîte my box.

Tiens-toi tranquille, enfant; comprends-tu? Be quiet, child; do you understand?

Oh, ciel! Que c'est beau! Oh, heaven! Isn't it beautiful!

tête-à-tête in private conversation.

nonnette nun.

et j'y tiens and I firmly believe it.

Il faut que je l'essaie! et à l'instant même! I must try it on! right now!

Est-ce que ma robe . . . vais danser! Do you like my dress? and my shoes? and my stockings? Watch, I'm going to dance!

Monsieur, je vous . . . monsieur? Sir, I thank you a million times for your generosity. Mother did it like this, didn't she, Sir?

comme cela like that.

grande passion a great love.

taille d'athlète athletic build.

Mon ange my angel.

croquant devouring.

voiture a carriage.

porte cochère a carriage entranceway.

vicomte a viscount.

beauté mâle male beauty.

fillette a little girl.

hâuteur arrogance.

Chapter 16

Summary

On the morning following the fire, Jane dreads seeing Rochester, but his behavior hasn't changed. Watching the servants cleaning Rochester's room, Jane is amazed to find Grace Poole sewing new curtain rings. Grace seems calm for a woman who tried to commit murder the previous night. Like the other servants, Grace seems to believe that Rochester fell asleep with his candle lit, and the curtains caught on fire. Grace advises Jane to bolt her door every night. Throughout their conversation, Grace gives no sign of guilt at having set the fire, astonishing Jane with her self-possession and hypocrisy. Jane is curious about Grace's role in the household. Why hasn't he fired Grace following the previous night's near murderous arson? At first, Jane believes Rochester might be in love with Grace, but rejects this idea because of Grace's unattractive and matronly appearance.

Jane is dismayed to learn that Rochester has left the house to attend a party at the Leas, home of Mr. Eshton, and will be gone for several days. She's particularly upset to learn that a beautiful woman, Miss Blanche Ingram, will be at the party. Recognizing that she's falling in love with Rochester, Jane tries to discipline her feelings by drawing two pictures: a self-portrait in crayon and an imaginary picture of Blanche on ivory. Whenever her feelings for Rochester become too intense, Jane compares her own plainness with Blanche's beauty.

Commentary

Jane's love for Rochester becomes apparent in this chapter. In her jealousy, Jane imagines a past love relationship between Grace and Rochester; perhaps Grace's "originality and strength of character" compensate for her lack of beauty. Jane doesn't think Rochester is overly impressed by women's looks; for example, Jane is not beautiful, yet Rochester's words, look, and voice on the previous night indicated that he likes her. But a major difference exists between Jane and Grace; as Bessie Leaven said, Jane is a lady. In fact, she looks even better than she did when Bessie saw her, because she has gained color, flesh, and vivacity from the pleasures she enjoys in her relationship with Rochester. She is especially pleased with her ability to vex and sooth him by turns, but always maintaining "every propriety of my station." All of these meditations show Jane's anxieties about Rochester hinge on the issues of social class and beauty.

Her hopes are dashed when she learns of Blanche Ingram. Considered the beauty of the county, Blanche, whose name means "fair" or "white," has "noble features," "raven-black" hair arranged in glossy curls, and brilliant black eyes, which contrast with the "pure white" clothes she wears. As with Jane's descriptions of Mrs. Reed and her son John, "darkness" often has negative connotations—the ethnocentricity of Victorian England tended to associate dark with night and evil. Therefore, Jane's description of Blanche, which emphasizes her dark, Spanish features, implies a negative side of her personality; like Céline, Blanche will be an unacceptable model of femininity. But at this point in the novel, Jane views Blanche as an accomplished and beautiful rival. Most important, as the daughter of landed gentry, her class position more closely matches Rochester's, making Jane's earlier claims to be a "lady" seem insignificant. Jane's dream of the previous night is quickly becoming reality: Rather than allow herself to be brutally tossed around in the sea of her passion for Rochester, Jane vows to be sensible and accept that Rochester could never love her. In creating contrasting portraits of herself and Blanche, Jane emphasizes her own plainness. To Blanche, on the other hand, she gives the loveliest face she can imagine, a Grecian neck, dazzling jewelry, and glistening satin. Once again, Jane's passions have become hyperbolic, as she cannot fully discipline her jealousy of Blanche. In her portraits, Jane excessively emphasizes the material differences between the two women, showing that Jane hasn't yet learned the value of her own spiritual superiority. Jane still has a long way to go on her path to self-knowledge.

Glossary

Qu'avez-vous . . . des cerises! What's wrong, Miss? your fingers tremble like a leaf, and your cheeks are red: as red as cherries!

ignis-fatuus a deceptive hope, goal, or influence; delusion. Literally, a strange light that sometimes appears over marshy ground.

Chapter 17

Summary

Jane is sickeningly disappointed when Rochester hasn't returned in a week, and Mrs. Fairfax suggests that he might go directly to Europe, not returning to Thornfield for a year or more. After two weeks, Rochester sends a letter telling Mrs. Fairfax that he will arrive in three days, along with a party of people. Jane is still amazed by Grace Poole's erratic behavior, yet no one else in the house seems to notice her odd habits, her isolation, or her drinking. One day, Jane overhears some of the servants discussing Grace, emphasizing how much Grace is being paid. From this conversation, Jane concludes that there is a mystery at Thornfield from which she is being purposely excluded.

On Thursday evening, Rochester and his guests arrive. Together, they give Jane an impression of upper-class elegance, unlike anything she has ever experienced. When Rochester summons Jane and Adèle to meet the party, Adèle is ecstatic, but Jane is nervous and remains inconspicuously in a window-seat. Jane gives her impressions of the guests, including the dark, majestic Blanche Ingram, whom she thinks Rochester must admire. Jane tries to sneak away from the party, but Rochester stops her. He notices she looks depressed and wonders why. At first he insists that she return to the drawing room, but when he sees tears in her eyes, he allows her to leave. In the future, though, she must appear in the drawing room every evening. He says goodnight, stopping himself from adding a term of endearment.

Commentary

In this chapter, the negative attributes of Blanche's character become apparent, at least in Jane's eyes. While Blanche's beauty lives up to Mrs. Fairfax's description of her, it also contains a "haughtiness," a "fierce and hard eye" that resembles her mother's. According to Jane, Blanche is "the very type of majesty." But majesty is hard to live with, and Jane wonders if Rochester truly admires her. Blanche appears to dislike both children—she notices Adèle with a "mocking eye"—and governesses. Her dislike of governesses goes beyond economizing: She rudely (because she knowingly speaks so Jane can hear her) calls them "detestable," "ridiculous" incubi, sucking the lifeblood from the family. Blanche's mother supports her, arguing "there are a thousand reasons why liaisons between governesses and tutors should never be tolerated a moment in any well-regulated house." Not only are these employees subject to constant persecution, but they are desexualized, not allowed to fall in love. Other members of the party join in with their stories of governess abuse; obviously, it was not pleasant to be responsible for teaching the children of the upper classes. The Ingrams' cruelty is similar to the Reeds', and Jane says Lady Ingram's "fierce and hard eye" reminds her of Mrs. Reed's.

Jane's gaze is active, almost masculine in this chapter: "I looked, and had an acute pleasure in looking—a precious yet poignant pleasure; pure gold, with a steely point of agony: a pleasure like what the thirst-perishing man might feel . . . ." Generally gazing is a power men have over women, appropriating women by looking at them, cataloguing their beauty. But here Jane appropriates that power for herself. While Blanche is looking for Rochester's gold coins, Jane finds her gold in gazing at her beloved. The mixture of pleasure and pain in her description—"poignant pleasure" and "steely point of agony"—suggest the erotic appeal of Rochester to her; this isn't an innocent glance, but a gaze tinged with sexual tension.

Glossary

passées out-of-style.

Elles changent de toilettes The women are changing their clothes.

Chez maman . . . comme cela on apprend. At my mother's house . . . when we had company, I followed them everywhere, to the drawing-room and their bedrooms; often I watched the maids fixing their ladies' hair or helping them dress, and it was very entertaining; I learned to imitate them.

Mais oui, mademoiselle: voilà cinq ou six heures que nous n'avons pas mangé. But of course, miss: We haven't eaten for five or six hours.

et alors quel dommage! that's too bad.

Est-ce que je ne puis . . . ma toilette. Can't I take one of these magnificent flowers, miss? It would complete my outfit.

minois chiffonné   darling; pretty face.

Bon jour, mesdames   good day, ladies.

père noble de théâtre   a grand patriarch of the theatre.

Tant pis   too bad.

charivari   clatter; noise.

belle passion   beautiful passion.

Au reste   besides.

Donna Bianca   Miss Blanche.

Signior   mister.

con spirito   with spirit.

Gardez-vous-en bien   take care.

Chapters 18 and 19

Summary

With guests at Thornfield, life is cheerful. One night, they are preparing for a game of charades. Rochester's group goes first, pantomiming a marriage ceremony with Rochester and Blanche as the happy couple. They then enact the story of Eliezer and Rebecca, and end with Rochester as a prisoner in chains. Colonel Dent's team correctly guesses the overall meaning of the three charades: Bridewell, an English prison. No longer interested in the charades, Jane watches the interactions between Rochester and Blanche. Their intimate style of conversing leads Jane to believe they will soon marry.

But Jane doesn't believe they love each other. Rochester is marrying for social and political reasons, while Blanche is marrying for money. Mr. Mason an old acquaintance of Rochester's, arrives one day. Jane immediately dislikes Mason's "unsettled and inanimate" face. From Mason, she learns that Rochester once lived in the West Indies.

A gypsy woman, old Mother Bunches, arrives from a nearby camp and wants to tell the fortunes of "the quality." Lady Ingram wants the old woman sent away, but Blanche insists upon having her fortune told. After fifteen minutes with the old woman, Blanche returns, and has obviously received disappointing news. Mary Ingram and Amy and Louisa Eschton have their fortunes read together and return laughing, impressed by Mother Bunches' intimate knowledge of their lives. Finally, the gypsy insists upon telling Jane's fortune. Jane isn't frightened, just interested and excited.

Jane enters the library and finds the gypsy woman seated snugly in an easy chair. She sits in front of the fire, reading something that looks like a Prayer Book. Despite Jane's protests to the contrary, the gypsy woman tells Jane she is cold, sick, and silly. Jane, she foretells, is very close to happiness; if Jane made a movement toward it, bliss would result. Soon the gypsy's speech has wrapped Jane in a dream-like state, and she is surprised by how well the old woman knows the secrets of her heart. The gypsy also explains that she (the gypsy) crushed Blanche's marriage hopes by suggesting Rochester isn't as wealthy as he seems.

The gypsy then reads each of Jane's features, as the voice drones on it eventually becomes Rochester's. Jane tells Rochester the disguise was unfair and admits she had suspected Grace Poole of being the masquerader. Before leaving, Jane tells Rochester about Mason's arrival; he is visibly upset by this news. Rochester worries that Mason has told them something grave or mysterious about him. Later that night she hears Rochester happily leading Mason to his room.

Commentary

Character
Insight

More aspects of Blanche Ingram's bad behavior are presented in this chapter. For example, she pushes Adèle away with "spiteful antipathy" and her treatment of Jane isn't much better: She "scorned to touch [Jane] with the hem of her robes as she passed" and quickly withdrew her eyes from Jane "as from an object too mean to merit observation." Jane concludes that Blanche is an inferior example of femininity because, like Céline Varens, she is showy, but not genuine. Her heart is "barren," her mind is "poor," and she lacks "freshness," the one trait Rochester claims to be searching for. Qualities Jane admires in women include force, fervor, kindness, and sense.

The chapter contains many prophetic events. Linking marriage with imprisonment, the charade foreshadows the circumstances of Rochester's marriage that has trapped him for life with a mad woman; Rochester is stuck in a "Bridewell" of his own creation. The arrival of Mr. Mason also prefigures change. Immediately disliking the tame vacancy of Mason's eyes, Jane compares him with Rochester, finding they differ like a gander and a falcon. Mason's difference lies in foreignness; recently arrived from the West Indies, Mason appears to suffer from a heat-induced languor. Mason will play a pivotal role in the plot of the story, and his presence provides another example of how foreigners are denigrated in this novel.

In posing as a gypsy woman, Rochester is assuming an ambiguous role—a position of both gender and class inferiority. In his disguise, he is almost denied admittance to his own home, and is referred to here by Jane as "mother" rather than "master." Many critics argue Jane's relationship with Rochester is marked by ambiguities of equality and independence: In their first meeting, for example, Rochester is dependent upon Jane to return to his horse. As gypsy woman, Rochester breaks gender boundaries and further aligns himself with mystical knowledge.

During this tale, Rochester wears a red cloak, connecting with other red images in the novel and showing his connection with the element of passion. Given the class differences between them, Rochester can't reveal his feeling for Jane in plain English, but must keep his words, like his face, veiled. As his language becomes plainer, more directly revealing the secrets of her heart, it paradoxically leads her not into reality, but into a dream state: Jane says the gypsy's strange talk leads Jane into "a web of mystification."

Character Insight

Rochester's almost supernatural powers are highlighted in this scene: His ability to weave a magical web around Jane with words and, more importantly, his ability to look almost directly into her heart so she feels an "unseen spirit had been sitting for weeks by my heart watching its workings and taking record of every pulse." He has also seen through Blanche's heart, recognizing her fortune-hunting mission. His witch's skill is being able to peer deeply into women's hearts, extracting their secrets: Notice that he does not tell the fortunes of any of the men in the party.

Glossary

Voilà Monsieur Rochester, qui revient! Look, it's Mr. Rochester returning!

surtout an overcoat.

le cas an occasion.

diablerie witchcraft.

ad infinitum endlessly.

Chapter 20

Summary

Later that evening, Jane lies in bed, gazing at the moonlight coming in her window. Suddenly, she hears a heart-stopping cry for help. Jane hurriedly puts on some clothes, horror shaking her body. All members of the party have gathered in the hallway, wondering if the house is on fire or if robbers have broken in. Rochester assures them that the noise was simply a servant having a bad dream and sends them back to their beds. Jane knows this is a lie, because she heard the strange cry, a struggle, and then a call for help. Before too long, Rochester knocks on her door, asking if she can help him, as long as she isn't afraid of blood. Together they climb to the mysterious third story of the house.

There they discover Richard Mason with a bloody arm. Rochester asks Jane to sop up the blood while he runs for the surgeon, but insists that Mason and Jane not speak with each other; if they do, Rochester will "not answer for the consequences." Jane stares at a cabinet in the room, which bears a grim design: the twelve Christian apostles with a dying Jesus hanging from a cross above them. As dawn approaches, Rochester finally returns with the surgeon. While he dresses Mason's wounds, the men speak obscurely of the woman who bit and stabbed Mason. Rochester has Jane run downstairs to find a special cordial he bought from an Italian charlatan. He measures twelve drops of the liquid into a glass, and has Mason drink the mixture, which Rochester claims will give him the "heart" he lacks for an hour or so.

After Mason has left, Jane and Rochester walk through the gardens. Rochester tells Jane the hypothetical story of a wild boy indulged from children, who commits a "capital error" while in a remote foreign country. He lives in debauchery for a while, then seeks to resume a happy, pure life with a kind stranger, but a "mere conventional impediment stands in his way." What would Jane do in such a situation, Rochester asks? Jane's answer is that a sinner's reformation should never depend on another person; instead, he should look to God for solace. Rochester then asks Jane, without parable, if marrying Blanche would bring him regeneration? He describes Blanche as a "strapper," big and buxom, like the women of Carthage, then rushes off to the stables to speak with Dent and Lynn.

Commentary

The secret residing on the third floor of Rochester's house is becoming ever more difficult for Rochester to disguise. Rochester's feelings are apparent through his description of his house; while for Jane it is a "splendid mansion," for Rochester it is a "mere dungeon," a Bridewell. While she sees only the glamour of the place, he sees the gilding as slime, the silk draperies as cobwebs, the marble as "sordid slate." Jane is unable to see below the surface to the secret residing within Rochester's domestic space. Under a veneer of domestic tranquility lies a monstrous secret—in the form of the strange woman who lives on the third floor. As Jane notes, this crime or mystery is one that can be neither "expelled nor subdued by the owner," emphasizing Rochester's inability to control this woman. Descriptions of her—she "worried me like a tigress" and "she sucked the blood: she said she'd drain my heart"—suggest her ferocious power and vampiric tendencies. Bertha seems to represent a silent rebellion brewing in women's minds, one Jane will discuss later in the novel.

Style & Language

Jane Eyre combines the techniques of several literary genre, including the bildungsroman (a novel that shows the psychological or moral development of the main character), the romance, and the gothic novel. Elements of gothic predominate in this chapter. Generally, gothic uses remote, gloomy settings, and a sinister, eerie atmosphere to create a feeling of horror and mystery. Jane's language in this chapter—filled with references to the supernatural, mystery, crime, secrets, and excessive emotions—fits this rubric. For example, Jane's description of her experience on the mysterious, remote third story of the house contributes to the reader's sense of horror and impending mystery: She tells of the "mystic cells," of "a pale and bloody spectacle," of a mystery that breaks out "now in fire and now in blood, at the deadest hours of night," creating a "web of horror." Her portrait of the grim cabinet depicting the twelve apostles, on which she imagines Judas "gathering life and threatening a revelation of Satan himself," suggests a devilish, supernatural evil. Similarly, Rochester's ability to conjure up a cordial to give Richard almost supernatural strength, hints at his mysterious, possibly unnatural powers.

Chapter 21

Summary

Jane remembers Bessie Leaven saying that dreams of children are a sign of trouble, either to oneself or one's kin. Jane is worried because she has been dreaming of infants for the past seven successive nights, including the night she was roused by Mason's cry. It also happens on the day Jane learns of her cousin John's death. The news of her son's death has caused Mrs. Reed to have a stroke, and she is now asking for Jane.

Jane arrives at Gateshead at five o'clock on May 1, greeted by Bessie, who prepares tea for them both. As they sit discussing old times, Jane realizes that the flame of her old resentments against the Reeds has been extinguished. She walks into the main house and meets her two cousins again: Eliza is tall and ascetic looking, while Georgiana is buxom and beautiful. Bessie takes Jane to see Mrs. Reed, whose face is as stern and restless as ever. While Jane would like to be reconciled with her aunt, Mrs. Reed won't relinquish her animosity. Jane learns the source of Mrs. Reed's anger toward her: Mrs. Reed was jealous of the relationship that Jane's mother, Mr. Reed's favorite sister, had with her husband, and of the fact that he showed Jane more attention than he ever showed his own children.

To pass the time, Jane sketches. Both Eliza and Georgiana are surprised with her skill, and Jane volunteers to draw their portraits. This breaks the ice between Jane and her cousins, and Georgiana begins confiding in her. Eliza is busy all day, every day; she plans to enter a convent when her mother dies. One rainy day, Jane sneaks upstairs to her aunt's room. Awaking from her lethargy, Mrs. Reed gives Jane a letter from her uncle, John Eyre. Written three years earlier, the letter reveals that he wishes to adopt Jane and leave her his fortune. Mrs. Reed didn't send it to Jane because she hated her too much and wanted to get revenge. One final time, Jane tries to seek reconciliation with her aunt, but Mrs. Reed refuses to forgive her. Her aunt dies at midnight.

Commentary

Character Insight

This chapter develops the characters of the Reeds, who haven't changed much in the years since Jane last saw them. The three Reed women are models of three different types of unacceptable female behavior. Eliza's ascetic appearance and crucifix signal her religious rebirth. Extremely rigid, Eliza has every aspect of her day planned out, yet Jane cannot find any "result of her diligence." When her mother dies, she plans to join a convent. Despite her seeming devotion, Eliza knows as little about compassion or love as does Mr. Brocklehurst. An angry, bitter woman, Eliza offers another negative image of Christianity. All of her work is self-centered, and she has little interest in her mother's health, not even shedding a tear when she dies. Always cold, rigid, impassible, Eliza is an example of a character who is too icy, too lacking in generous, passionate feeling. Jane's belief is that "judgement untempered by feeling is too bitter and husky a morsel for human deglutition"; Jane seeks a balance between judgment and feeling that will allow her a full, but healthy share in human joy.

While Eliza has too much judgment, too little feeling, Georgiana has the opposite: feeling without judgment. Where Eliza has consecrated herself to excessive asceticism, Georgiana has devoted herself to an immoderate fashionableness. Where Eliza is tall and extremely thin, Georgiana is buxom and voluptuous. Vain and shallow, Georgiana shows no interest in her brother's death or in her mother's illness. In a fashion similar to Céline Varens, Georgiana's mind is fully devoted to recollections of past parties and "aspirations after dissipations to come." Neither Eliza's nun-like life nor Georgiana's fashionable fluff interests Jane.

Aunt Reed is also a negative model. Refusing forgiveness or compassion, her aunt cherishes only ill feelings for Jane. While Jane's fiery passions have been extinguished, her aunt maintains a heated hatred for Jane until the moment of her death. In fact, she wishes Jane had died in the typhus outbreak at Lowood. This animosity is based on jealousy: She couldn't accept her husband's love of his sister or her child. Despite her attempts to keep John Eyre away from Jane, his repeated appearance in the story foreshadows his role later in her life, a role that will center on money. Aunt Reed's revenge attempt will be unsuccessful.

Chapter 22

Summary

Jane remains at Gateshead for a month, helping Georgiana and Eliza prepare for their departures: Georgiana to her uncle in London, and Eliza to a nunnery in Lisle, France. Eliza compliments Jane on her independence and hard work. The older Jane interrupts the narrative, telling Eliza's and Georgiana's futures: Eliza becomes the Mother Superior of a convent while Georgiana marries a wealthy, worn-out man of fashion. Mrs. Fairfax writes to Jane while she is at the Reeds, informing her that the house party has ended and that Rochester has gone to London to buy a new carriage, supposedly in anticipation of his upcoming marriage to Blanche.

Returning to Thornfield feels odd to Jane. She wonders where she'll go after Rochester marries and is impatient to see him again. Unexpectedly, she sees him sitting on a narrow stone stile, with a book and pencil in his hand. He teases her about sneaking up on him, like a "dream or shade." Almost against her will, Jane tells him that her only home is with him. At the house, Jane is warmly greeted by Mrs. Fairfax, Adèle, Sophie, and Leah, declaring there is no happiness like being loved. Over the next two weeks, Jane is surprised that no wedding preparations are being made, nor does Rochester journey to Ingram Park to visit Blanche. Never has she seen Rochester so happy; never has Jane loved him so well.

Commentary

In this chapter, Jane is again described as a magical creature. Indeed, the entire setting has become invested with magic. Walking on the road to Thornfield, Jane notices that the sky seems lit by fire, a spiritual "altar burning behind its screen of marbled vapour." When he sees her coming down the lane, Rochester wonders why she hasn't called a carriage "like a common mortal," but instead, steals home at twilight like a "dream or a shade." Similarly, when she declares she is returning from visiting her dead aunt, Rochester interprets her as saying she comes from the "other world—from the abode of people who are dead." If he had the courage, he would touch her to be sure she isn't "a substance or shadow" or elf. Touching her would be like touching one of the blue *ignis fatuus* lights in the marsh, a deceptive light that can't be found. In the same way, when she asks him whether he has been to London, Rochester wonders if she "found that out by second sight." Rochester wishes he could be more beautiful for his future bride, and asks fairy Jane for "a charm, or a philter" that would make him handsome, just as he earlier provided Richard Mason with a potion to make him fearless. In her admiration for Rochester, Jane believes a "loving eye is all the charm needed." That evening, Jane sits with Mrs. Fairfax and Adèle in the drawing room, and a "ring of golden peace" surrounds them. Their domestic happiness appears to be controlled by a magical power beyond their control, a magic circle of protection and repose, induced by Jane's prayers that they not be parted.

Jane isn't the only one with special powers. She reminds the reader of Rochester's ability to read her unspoken thoughts with incomprehensible acumen. In addition, his "wealth" of power for communicating happiness also seems magical. As she tries to leave him, an impulse holds her fast, "a force turned me round. I said—or something in me said for me, and in spite of me," wherever he is will be her home—her only home. In this instance, it's as if Rochester is compelling her to confess her feelings for him, and she can't possibly resist. Why is so much emphasis placed on both lover's otherworldly powers? The supernatural elements add to the gothic feel of the tale, and also make their love seem special, magical, like something existing outside of ordinary time and space.

Yet Jane isn't secure in her relationship with Rochester. Despite their obvious closeness, Jane still hears "a voice" warning her of near separation and grief. Her magical, psychic powers don't reveal a painless future. Similarly, she dreams of Miss Ingram closing the gates of Thornfield against her and sending her away, while Rochester smiles sardonically. As Rochester suggests, Jane seems to have a second sight, warning her of impending danger and separation from her beloved.

Glossary

bon soir good evening.

prête à croquer sa petite maman Anglaise ready to devour her little English mother.

Chapter 23

Summary

It is a beautiful midsummer's night. As the sun sets, Jane walks around the gardens of Thornfield, enjoying the solemn purple that colors the sky. Smelling Rochester's cigar from a window, Jane moves into the more secluded space of the orchard. But Rochester is now in the garden. Jane tries to escape unseen, but he speaks to her, asking her to look at an interesting moth. Although uncomfortable being alone with Rochester at night, Jane is unable to find a reasonable excuse for leaving him.

During their ensuing conversation, Rochester tells Jane she'll soon need to leave Thornfield forever because he's finally marrying Miss Ingram, whom he humorously calls "an extensive armful." Rochester teasingly tells her of a governess position, undertaking the education of the five daughters of Mrs. Dionysius O'Gall of Bitternutt Lodge in Ireland. Together they sit on a bench under a chestnut-tree to discuss Jane's trip. Now Rochester admits his strong feelings for Jane, and she reveals her love for him. He proposes marriage. At first Jane doesn't believe he's serious, but she reads the truth in his face and accepts his proposal. He savagely declares that God has sanctioned their union, so he doesn't care what society thinks of the relationship.

A flash of lightening sends them rushing home through the rain. They are soaked, and when Rochester helps her out of her coat, he kisses her repeatedly. Jane looks up to see Mrs. Fairfax watching, pale and amazed. During the night, lighting splits the great chestnut tree in two.

Commentary

Throughout this chapter, nature symbolically mimics Jane's feelings. Blissfully spending time with Rochester, Jane notices that "a band of Italian days had come from the South, like a flock of glorious passenger birds, and lighted to rest them on the cliffs of Albion." Everything is in its "dark prime," as the apex of Jane and Rochester's relationship is reached. On this splendid midsummer's evening, Jane notes the sky is "burning with the light of red jewel and furnace flame at one point"; the sky, like their love is passionate, flaming. Not a delicate white jewel, the heavens now glow with a fervent red. Ripe and blooming, the world offers various sensual pleasures; the gooseberry-tree is laden with fruit large as plums; the sweet-briar, jasmine, and rose have yielded a "sacrifice of incense"; Rochester tastes the ripe cherries as he walks through the garden; and the nightingale sings. This moment combines material pleasures with the spiritual pleasures of a "sacrifice of incense" and Jane's feeling that she could "haunt" the orchard forever.

But the world has changed by the end of the chapter: The chestnut tree under which Rochester proposed now ails, "writhing and groaning" in the roaring wind. Thunder and lightening crack and clash, so Jane and Rochester are forced to race back to the house in the pouring rain. The relationship has reached the zenith of ripeness, and a fallow, tragic time is on the way, symbolized by this raging storm. During the night, lighting splits the great chestnut tree, foreshadowing the separation that will soon befall Jane and Rochester.

The chapter also continues themes discussed earlier, such as the problems of class difference and the spiritual nature of their relationship. Early in their conversation, Rochester treats Jane like a good servant: Because she's been a "dependent" who has done "her duty," he, as her employer, wants to offer her assistance in finding a new job. Jane confirms her secondary status, referring to Rochester as "master," and believing "wealth, caste, custom" separate her from her beloved, even though she "naturally and inevitably" loves him. In this quote, Jane creates her love for Rochester as essential and uncontrollable, and, therefore, beyond the bounds of class. Similarly, Rochester argues that an almost magical cord connects him to Jane. Yet she also believes Rochester may be playing with her feelings, that he may see her as an automaton, "a machine without feelings"; because she is "poor, obscure, plain, and little," he may mistakenly think she is also "soulless and heartless." At this point, she speaks to him beyond the "medium of custom, conventionalities," even flesh, and her spirit addresses his spirit in a relationship of equality. Again, Jane creates equality by moving the relationship outside of the material world, and into the spiritual: At "God's feet," they can stand side-by-side, rather than with Rochester leading, Jane following.

Chapters 24 and 25

Summary

The next morning, Jane wakes, wondering if the previous night was just a dream. She feels transformed; even her face looks different, no longer plain. Believing Jane has taken an immoral turn, Mrs. Fairfax is cool and quiet at breakfast, but Jane feels she must let Rochester give explanations. When she walks up to the schoolroom in search of Adèle, Jane finds Rochester instead. He calls her "Jane Rochester," which she finds frightening, and tells her the wedding will be in four weeks. Jane doesn't believe the wedding will actually happen—it would be a "fairy-tale," too much happiness for a real human.

Rochester vows to make the world recognize Jane's beauty, but she worries that he's trying to transform her into a costumed ape. Jane is upset by Mrs. Fairfax's response to the news of the engagement. Rather than being delighted with the relationship, Mrs. Fairfax warns Jane to maintain a distance from Rochester, because she's worried about the differences between their ages and social classes. Later that day, Jane and Rochester drive to Millcote to make purchases for the wedding, and Adèle rides with them. They shop for silk and jewels, making Jane feel like a "doll." She vows to write her uncle in Madeira when she returns home, reasoning that she'd be more comfortable accepting Rochester's gifts if she knew she'd one day have her own money to contribute to the relationship. That evening, Rochester sings Jane a romantic song, but she has no intention of sinking into a "bathos of sentiment." She plans to keep her distance until after the wedding vows.

In Chapter 25, all of the preparations are ready for the wedding, which takes place the next day. Jane cannot bring herself to label her luggage with the cards that say "Mrs. Rochester," because this person doesn't yet exist. Together, they eat their last dinner at Thornfield before leaving on their European honeymoon. Jane can't eat, but tells Rochester about a strange occurrence that happened the previous night, while he was away: Before Jane went to bed, she discovered a hidden gift from Rochester—an expensive veil from London that she doubts can transform her from a plebian to a peeress. As she slept, she dreamt of a child, too young and feeble to walk, who cried in her arms. Rochester walked on a road ahead of her, but she was unable to catch him. The dream then took her to Thornfield Hall, which had become a "dreary ruin," with nothing remaining but a "shell-like wall." Trying to get a final glimpse of Rochester, she climbed the wall of Thornfield, but it collapsed, causing her to fall and drop the child. When she woke, she saw the figure of a woman in her room, someone she didn't recognize. The woman, whose face was ghastly, "savage," vampirish, threw Jane's veil over her own face. After gazing at herself in the mirror, the woman took the veil off, ripped it in two, and trampled it. Then the woman walked over to Jane's bed and peered into her face, causing her to faint for the second time in her life. When Jane woke in the morning, she discovered the veil on the floor, torn in two, so she knows the experience wasn't a dream.

Rochester thanks God that Jane wasn't harmed and then suggests that the woman must have been Grace Poole. In a state between sleeping and waking, Jane simply didn't recognize her. He promises to explain everything in "a year and a day" after their marriage. Rochester insists that Jane sleep in Adèle's bed this night, with the door securely fastened.

Commentary

Now that Jane has accepted Rochester's proposal, he seems intent on transforming her into the ideal object of affection. Already that morning, he has sent to London to have the family jewels sent to Thornfield for Jane, and he wants her to wear satin, lace, and priceless veils. Jane worries she'll lose herself if "tricked out" in these "stage-trappings." Not only does he want to make Jane a "beauty," Rochester also wants her to be his "angel" and "comforter." Jane reminds him that she simply wants to be herself, not some "celestial" being. A flaw has become apparent in Rochester's approach to love. While he claims to dislike fortune-hunting women, such as Céline Varens or Blanche Ingram, he seems to be trying to turn Jane into one of them. In fact, she argues that if she accepted his demands, he would soon grow tired of her. As "performing ape," Jane would be no better than a kept woman, an elegantly clothed object performing for her master. Instead, Jane wants to maintain both her personality and her independence. What Rochester values in Jane is her pliancy, which allows him to shape her into the woman he desires, something that wouldn't have been possible with a powerful woman like Blanche. Rochester still has much to learn about love.

Allusions to fairy tales continue in this chapter. Rochester tells Adèle that Jane is the fairy from Elf-land whose errand is to make him happy. This fantasy reminds the reader that one of Rochester's primary hopes from this marriage is that it will somehow purify him: For example, he wants to revisit all of his old haunts in Europe, tracing all of his old steps, but now "healed and cleansed" by his angelic Jane. By recreating her as fairy or angel, Rochester fulfills his own fantasy of magically erasing his past transgressions and beginning a fresh, new life.

Theme

But what does this fantasy offer Jane? Reduced to muse or "doll," Jane has no power over her own future. Jane makes this idea apparent when she claims Rochester gives her a smile such as a sultan would "bestow on a slave his gold and gems had enriched." Insisting that he prefers his "one little English girl" to the "Grand Turk's whole seraglio," Rochester points to Jane's powerlessness, her reduction to sex slave. Rather than becoming slave, Jane vows she will become a missionary, preaching liberty to women enslaved within harems. While her comments imply a Eurocentric understanding of eastern culture—the enlightened Englishwoman coming to the rescue of poor, imprisoned Turkish women—she insightfully implies that the position of English women isn't much better than that of their Turkish counterparts; both are enslaved by male despotism, which makes women objects of male desire, rather than thinking, independent subjects.

Literary Device

Chapter 25 is filled with prophetic symbols and dreams, as Brontë prepares the reader for the climactic Chapter 26, in which Jane discovers Rochester's secret. As in the previous chapter, nature reflects the coming tragedy. The wind blows fiercely and the moon is blood-red, reflecting an excess of passion. The cloven chestnut tree symbolically foreshadows Jane's future with Rochester, both their impending separation and their ultimate union. Jane's visions of Thornfield's desolation prefigure its charred remains after Bertha Mason torches it. Critics have often seen the child in Jane's dreams as a representation of Jane's fear of marriage or of childbearing. Throughout these chapters, Jane's anxieties about a loss of identity within her marriage are apparent. Thus, her dream of the small child, "too young and feeble to walk," could easily represent her immature self, unable to create an independent identity. When she tries to speak to Rochester, she is "fettered" and "inarticulate"—she feels she will have no power and no voice within the relationship.

As with previous changes in Jane's life, this one is foreshadowed not only by dreams, but also by the appearance of a ghostly apparition, Bertha Mason. This strange woman who rends the wedding-veil in two has been viewed by critics as Jane's double. While the powerless child reflects Jane's feelings of helplessness, Bertha shows Jane's rebellion. Bertha does Jane a favor—Jane didn't like the veil nor the sense that Rochester was trying to alter her identity by buying her expensive gifts, and her resistance is enacted through Bertha's actions. Bertha's vampiric appearance suggests that she is sucking away Rochester's lifeblood, but she also has a sexual power: The "blood-red" moon, a symbol of women's menstrual cycles, is reflected in her eyes. Like Blanche Ingram, Bertha is a woman Rochester can't control, a woman with "savage" and, probably sexual, power. Small and naïve, Jane can't compete with these women. In the final image of this scene, Jane curls up in bed with Adèle—significantly, Rochester has suggested Jane spend the night locked in the nursery, once again emphasizing her childish, dependent status and his desperate attempts to shelter her from Bertha's potent and sexualized rage.

Glossary

sans mademoiselle? without Miss?

Oh, qu'elle y sera mal—peu confortable! Oh, things will be unpleasant for her there—uncomfortable!

un vrai menteur a real liar.

conte de fée a fairy-tale.

du reste, il n'y avait pas de fées, et quand même il y en avait besides, there were no fairies there, and even if there were.

pour me donner une contenance for me to give myself airs.

tête-à-tête an intimate conversation.

Chapter 26

Summary

At seven o'clock on Jane's wedding day, Sophie arrives to help her dress. Jane wears the plain blond veil she has made herself, rather than the fancy veil that was destroyed by Bertha. In her wedding dress, Jane looks so different from her usual self that she seems a stranger to herself. As they drive to the church, Rochester looks grim, and Jane is so nervous that she doesn't notice whether the day is fair or foul. In the cemetery near the church, Jane observes two strangers and sees them again in the shadows of the church. When the clergyman is about to ask Rochester whether he takes Jane for his wife, a voice declares the wedding can't continue because of an "impediment." Rochester has another wife who is still living: Bertha Antoinetta Mason, a Creole woman he married fifteen years ago in Jamaica. Richard Mason appears, confirming this evidence, and Rochester admits that he had planned to commit bigamy.

Rochester commands everyone back to Thornfield to see his wife. Refusing to let go of Jane's hand, Rochester leads her up to the secret room on the third floor. They find Bertha groveling on all fours, running backwards and forwards like a beast. Her hair, wild as an animal's mane, hides her face. The woman attacks Rochester, almost throttling him, until finally he binds her to a chair.

Briggs surprises Jane by telling her that her uncle, John Eyre, had alerted Richard Mason to the marriage. John Eyre is a business associate of Mason's, so when Jane's letter arrived, announcing her engagement, he shared the information with Mason, who was resting in Madeira on his return voyage to Jamaica. John Eyre was dying and couldn't return to England to rescue Jane, so he sent Mason instead. Everyone leaves the attic, and Jane locks herself in her room. All her hopes are dead. In this moment of despair, Jane returns to God, silently praying that he remain with her.

Commentary

Rochester's secret has been revealed. In the previous chapter, Bertha was merely an apparition; in this one, she becomes fully flesh and blood. An insane, Creole woman, Bertha represents British fears of both foreigners and women. Part human, part beast, Bertha is Jane's double, representing all of her rage and anger over the loss of identity the marriage promises to bring. Unlike Jane, who submissively gives in to Rochester's demands, Bertha refuses to be controlled; a woman whose stature almost equals her husband's, she fights with him, showing a "virile" force that almost masters the athletic Rochester. Finally, she is roped to a chair, much as Jane almost was in the incident in the red-room. Post-colonialist critics, such as Gayatri Spivak, have argued that Bertha, the foreign woman, is sacrificed so that British Jane can achieve self-identity, and the novelist Jean Rhys has written a novel called *The Wide Sargasso Sea* that presents Bertha's life in Jamaica before her madness. Both of these women writers suggest Rochester's relationship with Bertha wasn't as innocent as he claims; as a colonialist, he was in Jamaica to make money and to overpower colonized women. In the nineteenth-century, men had almost complete legal power over women, and perhaps this lack of power contributed to Bertha's madness, just as it caused Jane's temporary insanity in the red-room. These critics remind the reader that *Jane Eyre* isn't merely a story critiquing the social injustices against women, but also exposing the brutality of colonialism. In the previous chapter, Jane had joked about leading a rebellion of the women in Rochester's imaginary seraglio; now she has almost become a member of that harem, but Bertha leads the resistance.

Brontë's use of ice imagery in this chapter contrasts with the fiery images of the previous few chapters. In Chapter 25, for example, the wild wind and blood-red moon symbolized Jane's passion, but here all of that energy has drained away. Bertha's red eyes and virile force emphasize her excessive, crazy passions, but Jane has become a husk. Gone is the "ardent, expectant woman," and in her place is the "cold, solitary girl again." Jane imagines nature mimicking her desolation and chill: a Christmas frost has whirled through June, and "ice glazed the ripe apples, drifts crushed the blowing roses; on hayfield and cornfield lay a frozen shroud." All the world has symbolically become icy, frozen, snowy in sympathy with Jane's dead hopes. For Jane, the world has become a white waste, a chill, stark corpse that will never revive.

Chapter 27

Summary

Later that afternoon, Jane awakes, wondering what she should do: Leave Thornfield at once is the answer. At first, she doesn't think she can leave Rochester, but an inner voice tells her she both can and should. Jane leaves her room, tripping over Rochester, who sits in a chair outside the door. He carries her down to the library, offering her wine and food. Rochester plans to lock Thornfield up, send Adèle away to school, and escape with Jane to a villa in the south of France, where they would live "both virtually and nominally" as husband and wife. Jane won't accept his logic; if she lived with him, she would be his mistress, a position she doesn't want. Afraid of his passionate nature, Jane calls to God for help.

Rochester tells Jane the history of his family: His greedy father left all of his estate to Rochester's older brother Rowland, so that the property wouldn't be divided. When Rochester left college, he was sent to Jamaica to marry Bertha, who supposedly would receive a fortune of thirty thousand pounds. Bertha was a beautiful woman, tall and majestic like Blanche Ingram. Bertha seemed to be a dazzling woman and Rochester was aroused by her. He mistook this lust for love. Before he knew it, they were married. After the honeymoon, Rochester learned that Bertha's mother was shut in an asylum and her younger brother was mentally challenged. Ultimately, Bertha's excesses led her into premature insanity. Rochester contemplates suicide, but then decides to return to Europe with Bertha. Both his father and brother are dead, and no one else knows of his marriage. Rochester spends the next ten years searching for a woman to love, but finds only mistresses. From his story, Jane realizes she can never live with Rochester; she would become simply another of his now-despised mistresses.

That night, Jane dreams her mother, transformed from the moon, whispers into her heart, "My daughter, flee temptation." Jane does. She packs up a few trinkets, grabs her purse, which contains a mere twenty shillings, and steals away. Walking past Rochester's room, Jane knows she could find a "temporary heaven" there, but she refuses to accept it. Instead, she sneaks out of the house, beginning a journey far away from Thornfield.

Commentary

In this chapter, Jane learns more about Rochester's past, particularly his relationship with Bertha. Much of this information hinges on the problem of excessive sexuality. As Rochester constantly reminds Jane, he is not "cool and dispassionate"; instead, he seems to devour her with his "flaming glance." His passionate nature seems to have contributed to his marriage, and to his current problems. When he first arrived in Spanish Town, Rochester found Bertha dazzling, splendid, and lavish, all qualities that excited his senses. But he soon discovers that she is sexually excessive: "coarse," "perverse," "intemperate," and "unchaste." Rochester implicitly suggests his inability to control Bertha then (as now) hinges on her sexuality: She chose her own sexual partners, refusing to maintain the monogamy required by British moral standards. While he criticizes Bertha's sexual excess, Rochester participates in his own with his three mistresses—Céline, Giacinta, and Clara—and his current attempt to make Jane part of the harem. When he tries to accuse Jane of flinging him back to "lust for a passion—vice for an occupation," she reminds him that these are his choices. She senses that his passion is out of control—he's in a "fury" and glowing like a furnace, with "fire" flashing from his eyes—and Jane needs to walk away from the relationship until he has learned self-control and until she can enter the relationship on a more equal footing.

These are not lessons Jane wants to learn. To keep herself from the "temporary heaven" of Rochester's bedroom, Jane hears prophetic voices that guide her on the path of moral righteousness. When the chapter begins, a voice instructs her to leave Thornfield at once. Later, a kinder voice, the moon transformed into the "white human form" of her mother, insists she flee the temptations in Rochester's thorny field. Therefore, Jane sets out on the next stage of her quest: to regain her personal identity, almost lost through her consuming passion for Rochester. Significantly, when she leaves Thornfield, Jane takes only a few trinkets with her—no extra clothes, nothing to remind her of her past life, nothing associated with the "visionary" bride she had almost become. Jane is slowly stripping herself down to nothing, so she'll be able to rebuild herself from nothing. Her future is now "an awful blank: something like the world when the deluge was gone by." Just like the passengers on Noah's Ark after the rains subsided, Jane is beginning life with nothing but a great emptiness.

Chapters 28 and 29

Summary

Two days later, the coachman drops Jane off in Whitcross. He couldn't take her any farther because she has run out of money. Accidentally, Jane leaves her packet in the coach and is now destitute. Nature is Jane's only relative, the "universal mother" who will lodge her without money, so Jane spends the night sleeping on the heath. Too hurt by memories of her broken heart to sleep, Jane rises, kneeling in the night, and prays to God. The next morning, she follows the road past Whitcross. Walking to the point of fatigue, she finally finds a town and enters a bakery to beg for bread or a job. No one will help her, and even the parson is away, at Marsh End, due to the sudden death of his father. Finally, she finds a farmer who gives her a slice of brown bread.

That night, Jane is unable to sleep peacefully in the woods. The only food she eats the next day is a pot of cold porridge that a little girl was about to throw into a pig trough. Across the moors, she suddenly sees the light of a house. Jane follows a road leading to the house, and enters its gate, peering in the lighted window. Inside she sees a well-kept house, a rough-looking elderly woman, and two graceful ladies dressed in mourning. The women are waiting for their brother, St. John, to return home. These cultivated young women, named Diana and Mary Rivers, are practicing their German. Jane knocks on the door, but the old servant, Hannah, turns her away. St. John overhears the conversation and offers Jane shelter because he thinks she's "a peculiar case." The Rivers offer her bread and milk and allow her to stay for the night. Jane tells them her name is "Jane Elliott."

Jane spends three days and nights in bed. Diana and Mary are happy to have taken her in, believing she would have died if they had left her outside. Looking at Jane, they conclude that she is well educated, because nothing in her appearance indicates "vulgarity or degradation." On the fourth day, Jane rises and dresses in her freshly washed clothes; she is once again clean and respectable, with no traces of dirt or disorder in her appearance. Jane goes downstairs and works in the kitchen with Hannah, from whom she learns that the house is called Marsh End or Moor House and is owned by the Rivers. Jane lectures Hannah for unfairly judging the poor, and Hannah begs Jane's forgiveness for initially denying her entrance to the house; the two women slowly become friends. From Hannah, Jane discovers that the Rivers are an "ancient" family. Several years ago, their father lost much money when a man he trusted went bankrupt, so Diana and Mary were forced to find work as governesses. Mr. Rivers died three weeks earlier of a stroke.

Jane tells the Rivers some of her history. The reason for her departure from her governess position she doesn't reveal, but assures them that she was blameless in the situation. She tells them Jane Elliott isn't her real name. Knowing Jane won't want to accept their charity for long, St. John promises to find her some unglamorous job.

Commentary

Jane has reached the dark night of her soul. Leaving the carriage that has brought her to Whitcross, Jane has nothing but the clothes she's wearing. Before beginning the final section of her journey of self-discovery, Jane must strip herself of all connections with humanity and rediscover her spiritual self. In some ways, this separation from society may be her punishment for the passion that elevated Rochester above God in her imagination and for her near participation in a bigamous relationship. Nature becomes Jane's mother, and she seeks repose at this great mother's breast. For her, nature is "benign and good," a safe mother who loves Jane, even though she's an outcast. Closely aligned with nature is God, whom Jane realizes is everywhere: At those moments when closest to nature, "we read clearest His infinitude, His omnipotence, His omnipresence." Like nature, Jane's God is filled with bounty, compassion, and forgiveness. The difference between Jane's loving God, and the malicious, demanding Christ of Mr. Brocklehurst or Eliza Reed is apparent. Nor is Jane's God similar to Helen Burns.' While Helen's God taught her to savor heaven over earth, Jane's God is closer to a pagan spirit, who offers both spirituality and material comfort. Jane wishes she could live in and on the natural world, but she can't. Instead, she must return to the company of humans to find food and permanent shelter. But her experience in the wilderness has begun to repair her damaged spirit.

**Character
Insight**

Jane's return to the human world is difficult. Penniless and dirty, she discovers that beggars are often objects of suspicion, and "a well-dressed beggar inevitably so." Because she doesn't fit into any class, neither a "real" beggar nor a "real" lady, Jane is outside of society's pre-ordained categories, and therefore, is viewed with mistrust and rejection. As Hannah says, "You are not what you ought to be, or you wouldn't make such a noise." Hannah implies that moral transgression is the only answer for the question of Jane's destitute position. In some sense, she's right. By placing her love for Rochester above all spiritual concerns, Jane has in some ways transgressed, and her present journey charts the process of her atonement. Washed of all sins by her night on the dewy moors, Jane is now ready to reenter human community. Peering through the window of the house on the moors, Jane sees an idyllic world. Unlike the stateliness of Thornfield, in which Jane felt inferior, the rustic simplicity of this cottage is comforting. Diana and Mary, serene, intelligent, and graceful, are the models of femininity that Jane seeks, and Jane is comforted by their "power and goodness." Similarly, St. John's willingness to allow an unknown beggar into his home suggests compassion, something Jane hasn't often known. As she crosses the threshold of his house, Jane no longer feels an "outcast, vagrant, and disowned by the wide world." She is able to put aside the character of mendicant and resume her "natural manner and character"; she says, "I began once more to know myself." Jane's dark night has ended: She lost herself on the moors but has rediscovered herself in the comfort of the Rivers' home.

Jane has reached the final destination on her journey of discovery; significantly, the house is called Marsh End, as Jane has reached the end of her march. This chapter develops the personalities of the residents at Marsh End. The housekeeper, Hannah, has been with the family for thirty years and works hard to protect Diana and Mary. Hannah admits she has no respect for Jane, because she has neither money nor a home. This class prejudice angers Jane, who reminds Hannah that poverty is no sin; in fact, many of the best people, such as Christ, lived destitute, and a good Christian shouldn't reject the poor. In this section, Jane recognizes the spiritual value of her experience of absolute poverty, which has stripped her of all markings of class. Now, however, she rejects the label of "beggar," showing that she, like Hannah, has prejudices against those who beg for a living. Jane has been careful to erase all signs of dirt and "disorder" from her appearance, so she can resume her proper identity. Similarly, the record she provides of Diana and Mary's conversations about her as she slept emphasizes her ladylike appearance: she is educated, her accent is pure, and her appearance doesn't indicate decadence. While Jane warns Hannah not to judge the poor, Jane is careful to erase all marks of poverty from her own appearance.

From Hannah, Jane discovers that the Rivers are ancient gentry, class-related information that will be important to Jane later in the novel. Their superiority is evident in Diana's and Mary's appearances and manners. Both women are charming, pretty, and intelligent, although Mary is more reserved than the more willful Diana. Like Miss Temple, these women provide Jane with a model of compassionate, refined, intellectually stimulating, and morally superior femininity that contrasts with the capriciousness of the Reeds and the self-centeredness of Blanche Ingram. St. John River's appearance also indicates a moral and intellectual superiority. According to Jane, his face's pure outline is Greek, and he has "a straight, classic nose; quite an Athenian mouth and chin." St. John's classic, handsome features contrast with Rochester's rugged appearance. The two men are like ice and fire. While St. John's blue eyes and ivory skin align him with ice, Rochester's dark hair and passionate nature connect him with fire. Jane immediately detects a restlessness or hardness under St. John's seemingly placid face, however. The differences between the two men will be further developed as the novel progresses.

Glossary

Da trat hervor Einer, anzusehen wie sie Sternen Nacht. Only one person came forward, to be watched like a crystal clear night.

Ich wäge ... Grimms. I weigh my thoughts on a small scale, my temper and behavior with weights the size of my outburst.

Deutsch German.

bairn a child.

alias an assumed name.

Chapter 30

Summary

After a few days, Jane has recovered her health enough to sit up and walk outdoors. Her conversations with Diana and Mary revive and refresh Jane, because their values and interests are so perfectly aligned with hers. Diana and Mary are better read than Jane, and Jane eagerly devours all the books they lend her. Drawing is the only area in which Jane's skill surpasses theirs. The intimacy Jane feels with the women doesn't extend to St. John, partly because he is often away from home, visiting the sick, and partly because his nature is so reserved and brooding.

A month passes. Diana and Mary prepare to return to their positions as governesses in a large, fashionable city in the south of England. Jane wonders if St. John has found any employment for her? Since he is "poor and obscure," he says he has only been able to devise an insignificant post for Jane—if she wants it, she can run a school for poor girls in Morton. Her salary would be thirty pounds, and she would have a furnished cottage to live in, provided by Miss Oliver, the only daughter of the rich owner of a needle factory and iron foundry. Although humble, the position's independence and safety appeal to Jane. St. John guesses that Jane won't remain long in Morton, because she'll soon long for society and stimulus. But St. John has a similar "fever in his vitals," as Diana reveals, and they know he will soon leave England. As the women sit talking, St. John enters the room, and announces their Uncle John has died, leaving all of his fortune to another relative. Their uncle and father had quarreled, and it was John's fault that Mr. Rivers lost most of his property and money.

Commentary

The "dark and hoary" appearance of Moor House seems to match Jane's psychology at this point of the novel; she has moved from Thornfield's luxury to Marsh End's natural and rugged beauty. Describing the environment around the house, Jane emphasizes its rustic, hardy feel: The fierce mountain winds have caused the trees to grow "aslant"; only the hardiest flowers bloom near it; and it is surrounded by some the "wildest little pasture-fields that ever bordered a wilderness of heath."

Theme

In this chapter, Jane emphasizes her intellectual affinity for the Rivers sisters. Being in their presence rekindles Jane's joy in learning, and the three women mutually share and bolster each other's skills; Diana teaches Jane German, while Jane offers Mary drawing lessons. As in earlier chapters, Jane here emphasizes the incongruity of the position of governesses. Although the Rivers sisters are members of an ancient and esteemed family that has fallen on hard times, they must spend their lives as the "humble dependents" of wealthy and haughty families who cannot fully appreciate their talents. For these families, Diana's and Mary's skills are comparable to those of their cook or waiting-woman. Brontë's depiction of the Rivers is probably based on personal experience. Like them, she was forced to work as a governess for a family she despised; like them, she took time to learn new languages so that she could increase her wages and open up a school of her own. Sadly, her attempt to open a school failed miserably, as not a single student applied for admittance.

While the Rivers girls are depicted favorably, Jane's feelings for St. John are more conflicted. His reserve and brooding suggest a troubled nature, and his zealous Christianity offers him neither serenity nor contentment. St. John's real nature is revealed in his sermon—Jane is unable to render accurately its effect on her. While St. John's tone is calm throughout, his nervous words have a "strictly restrained zeal" that reflects his bitterness and lack of "consolatory gentleness." His doom and gloom leave Jane feeling inexpressibly sad, because she feels his eloquence is born of disappointment. Jane compares his despair to her own regrets at the loss of her heaven with Rochester. Despite St. John's strictness, or perhaps because of it, he has not found the peace in God that reassured Jane during her awful night on the moors. Instead, St. John dwells on his poverty and obscurity, always looking for a way to become the hero he longs to be. Again, his difference from Rochester is apparent; while Rochester vents his passions, St. John hides his in "a fever in his vitals."

The death of their Uncle John is also significant. The astute reader will remember that Jane also had an uncle named John, one who was too ill to save her from Rochester's bigamous plot. The connections between the families will grow in the remainder of the novel.

Chapter 31

Summary

Jane has moved to her new home: the schoolroom cottage at Morton. Classes begin with twenty students; only three can read and none can write or do arithmetic. Some are docile and want to learn, while others are rough and unruly. Rather than feeling proud of her work, Jane feels degraded. She knows these feelings are wrong and plans to change them. Did she make the right decision, Jane wonders? Is it better to be a "free and honest" village schoolmistress or Rochester's mistress?

St. John interrupts Jane's reverie to offer her a gift from his sisters: a watercolor box, pencils, and paper. Jane assures him that she's happy with her new position. Seeing that Jane's discontent, he tells her his story. He, too, felt he had made a mistake by entering the ministry and longed for an exciting literary or political career, a profession that might bring him glory, fame, and power. Then one day he heard God's call, telling him to become a missionary, work requiring the best skills of the soldier, statesman, and orator. St. John has only to cut one more human tie and he will leave for India to fulfill his dream.

After he says this, their conversation is interrupted by the arrival of a beautiful young woman dressed in pure white: Rosamond Oliver. Jane wonders what St. John thinks of this "earthly angel"? Given the sudden fire she sees in his eye, Jane imagines he must be in love with Rosamond.

Commentary

Although Jane was quick to point out Hannah's class prejudices in Chapter 29, in this chapter Jane shows a lack of feeling for the peasants who are now her students. Jane chose this position, in part, to avoid becoming a governess/servant in the house of a rich family. Having met her uncultured students, Jane wonders if she has taken a step down the social ladder. Interestingly, when weighing her options in this chapter, Jane seems to have forgotten about the possibility of being a governess. Instead, she meditates on the merits of being caught in a "silken snare" as Rochester's mistress in the "fool's paradise at Marseilles," or of being "free and honest" as village schoolmistress in the "healthy heart of England." As before, a trade-off is made between the purity of England and the corruption of Europe; the British must go abroad to live out their illicit loves. Chastising herself for her criticism of her pupils, Jane tries not to forget that their "flesh and blood" is as good as that of the wealthy, and that the "germs of native excellence, refinement, intelligence, kind feeling, are as likely to exist in their hearts as in those of the best born." Jane's duty will be to develop the "germs," to transform the manners of the lower classes so they conform to upper-class standards of proper behavior. To St. John, Jane claims to be content to have friends, a home, and a job, when only five weeks earlier she was an outcast and beggar. Yet the seeds of her discontent are growing here, as they did at Lowood.

Character Insight

The chapter also develops St. John's personality. As Jane had guessed, he is riddled by restlessness and despair. Rather than becoming a priest, St. John would like to have been a politician, author, orator—any position that brought the possibility of glory, fame, and power. Instead, he is the clergyman for a poor and obscure parish. His solution is to become a missionary. Just as Jane retrains the minds of the lower classes in England, he will reform the values of the pagans in India. Both characters perpetuate a belief in British, Christian superiority. Both also confirm the supposed moral superiority of the upper classes. For instance, despite her documentation of the faults of the upper classes, she still seems to associate "refinement" and "intelligence" with the gentry, and "coarseness" and "ignorance" with the peasants. The iciness of St. John's character becomes more pronounced when he declares his intention to leave Morton after "an entanglement or two of the feelings" has been "broken through or cut asunder." This entanglement arrives in the form of Rosamond Oliver, who has "as sweet features as ever the intemperate clime of Albion moulded." Rosamond is the icon of British beauty and in love with St. John, yet he rejects her. While her appearance incites St. John like a thunderbolt, though he flushes and kindles at the sight of her petting his dog, St. John would rather turn himself into "an automaton," than succumb to her beauty or fortune. His ambition to forge a heroic career cuts St. John off from all deep human emotions. Perhaps, then, his religious zeal is the result of his repressed sexual feelings.

Chapter 32

Summary

After working with her students for a while, Jane discovers some intelligence among them. Jane is even surprised by their progress and begins personally to like some of the girls—and they like her. Jane teaches them grammar, geography, history, and needlework. Despite her popularity within the community and her growing happiness with her job, Jane is still troubled by strange dreams at night in which she always meets Rochester. Rosamond Oliver visits the school almost every day, usually when St. John is giving his daily catechism lesson. Although he knows Rosamond loves him, and he obviously loves her, St. John is not willing to sacrifice his heavenly ambition for worldly pleasure. When Rosamond learns that Jane can draw, she asks her to make a portrait.

St. John visits Jane while she is working on Rosamond's portrait. He has brought her a book of poetry, Sir Walter Scott's *Marmion*. While St. John gazes at Rosamond's picture, Jane offers to make him a copy, then, being bold, she suggests that he marry Rosamond at once. For exactly fifteen minutes, St. John imagines himself yielding to Rosamond, allowing human love to overwhelm him with its pleasures. Although St. John loves Rosamond wildly, he knows she wouldn't be a good wife for him, and he'd probably tire of her in twelve months. Rosamond wouldn't make an effective missionary's wife, and St. John isn't willing to relinquish his goals, because he is a cold, hard, ambitious man. As they sit talking, St. John suddenly notices something on Jane's blank piece of paper. She doesn't know what it is, but he snatches the paper, then shoots Jane a "peculiar" and "inexpressible" glance. He replaces the paper, tearing a narrow slip from the margin, then bids Jane "good-afternoon."

Commentary

Both Jane and St. John suffer from unrequited love in this chapter. While Jane is pleased with her "useful existence," she isn't fully satisfied with her new, safe life, and her repressed desires manifest at night in strange dreams: "dreams many-coloured, agitated, full of the ideal, the stirring, the stormy." Filled with adventure and romance, these dreams often lead her to Rochester. Similarly, St. John's "repressed fervour" for Rosamond shows in a subtle glow in this "marble-seeming features." A statesman, priest, and poet, St. John is unable to limit himself to a single passion or to "renounce his wide field of mission warfare" for the tamer pleasures of love. For St. John, missionary work won't involve compassion or joy, but "warfare."

This chapter also provides us with a short explanation of the role of art in modern life. Looking at the copy of Sir Walter Scott's poem *Marmion*, Jane calls it "one of those genuine productions so often vouchsafed to the fortunate public of those days—the golden age of modern literature." Scott's poetry belonged in the era of Romanticism, and it isn't surprising Jane should view the Romantics as the ideal of modern literature. Her own narrative inherits many themes and landscapes from them: the hills and moors of Scott and the romantic and passionate hero of Byron. In the Victorian era, the artist seemed in danger of becoming caught in the capitalist marketplace, as the industrial revolution ushered in a new focus on profitability. Jane assures her reader that neither poetry nor genius are dead, "nor has Mammon gained power over either, to bind or slay." Even in a capitalist age, art will maintain its freedom and strength: "they not only live, but reign and redeem: and without their divine influence spread everywhere, you would be in hell—the hell of your own meanness." These quotes indicate Brontë's own anxieties about the position of the artist in the modern world, yet she vehemently maintains art's spiritual power, which keeps it separate from mundane contamination. Art and genius are "[p]owerful angels, safe in heaven" that will redeem and enlighten.

Glossary

lusus naturae a freak of nature; something with some abnormal characteristic. [Latin]

Cui bono? To what good? [Latin]

Chapter 33

Summary

While a snowstorm whirls outside, Jane sits reading *Marmion*. Suddenly, she hears a noise at the door: it's St. John. After a long delay, he tells Jane's own story, ending by saying that finding Jane Eyre has become a matter of serious urgency. St. John explains that he discovered her true identity from the paper he tore from her art supplies, which had the name Jane Eyre inscribed on it. The reason everyone has been looking for Jane is that her uncle, Mr. Eyre of Madeira, is dead and has left his entire fortune to her, so she is now rich. Jane is astonished to learn she has inherited twenty thousand pounds and wishes she had a family to share it with.

As St. John prepares to leave, Jane asks why Mr. Briggs, Eyre's attorney, sent him a letter inquiring about Jane's whereabouts. St. John completes the story: his full name is St. John Eyre Rivers, so the Rivers are Jane's cousins. Jane feels she's found a brother and two sisters to love and admire; relatives, in her opinion, are real wealth, "wealth to the heart." Now she has the opportunity to benefit those who saved her life. She decides to share her legacy with them, to divide it into four pieces, making five thousand pounds each. That way, justice will be done, and Jane will have a home and family. St. John reminds her of the lofty place she could take in society with twenty thousand pounds, but Jane insists that she'd rather have love.

Commentary

This chapter highlights the differences in personality between Jane and St. John; while he is so cold "no fervour infects" him, Jane is "hot, and fire dissolves ice." For icy St. John, reason is more important than feeling, but for fiery Jane, feeling predominates. Relating her story, St. John expects Jane's primary concern will be to know why Briggs has been searching for her; instead, she's more interested in Rochester's fate, worrying that he has returned to his life of dissipation in Europe. After learning of the inheritance, Jane is sorry to hear her uncle, a man she's never met, is dead, and wishes she had a "rejoicing family" to share the money with, rather than her isolated self. So discovering she has three cousins is heavenly for Jane. In fact, the blessing of relatives is "exhilarating—not like the ponderous gift of gold: rich and welcome enough in its way, but sobering from its weight." St. John believes Jane is neglecting the essential points (the money) for the trifles (family). For a clergyman, St. John's lack of understanding of or caring for people is shocking. Sharing the wealth, Jane will transform it from an unwanted weight into a "legacy of life, hope, enjoyment," but her comment that the money will help her win "to myself lifelong friends," sounds as if she is planning to buy friendship with the legacy. Jane says she is happy to indulge her feelings, something she seldom has the opportunity to do. Jane values family and feeling above all else, while St. John thinks only of the opportunities, if she keeps the inheritance, that Jane will have to take her place in society.

Describing his love for his sisters at the end of the chapter, St. John says his affection for them is based on "respect for their worth, and admiration of their talents," and he believes he'll be able to love Jane because she also has "principle and mind." How cold his description of love is compared with Jane's passionate connection to Rochester, with her heartfelt "craving" for love and family. Her inheritance may lead Jane back to her relationship with Rochester. Earlier in the novel, as she planned her wedding, Jane worried because she couldn't offer Rochester beauty, money, or connections; now she has at least two of the three— relatives she's proud of and plenty of cash! Slowly, she is moving into a position of equality with Rochester.

Chapter 34

Summary

Christmas has arrived and Jane is closing the Morton school. She is happy to discover that she is beloved by the girls and promises to visit the school for an hour each week. St. John asks Jane if she wouldn't like to dedicate her life to working with the poor, but she wants to enjoy herself, as well as cultivating others. Jane sets off for Moor House to prepare for the arrival of Diana and Mary.

St. John shows a disappointing lack of interest in the renovations Jane has done at Moor House, but Diana and Mary ungrudgingly appreciate Jane's hard work. The women spend the week in "merry domestic dissipation," a pleasure St. John can't enjoy. He tells them Rosamond Oliver is to be married to a Mr. Granby, but the news doesn't seem to upset him. To Jane, St. John seems more distant than before they knew they were cousins.

One day when Jane sits home with a cold, St. John suddenly asks her to give up German lessons and learn Hindustani, the language he is studying in preparation for his missionary work. Slowly, St. John takes more control over Jane, sucking away her freedom; she doesn't enjoy her new servitude. She is also stricken with sadness, because she is unable to discover what has happened to Rochester since she left him. Then St. John surprises her. In six weeks, St. John will leave for India, and he wants Jane to accompany him, as his wife. If she goes to India, Jane knows she'll die prematurely, but she agrees to go anyway—if she can go as his sister, not his wife, because they don't love each other as husband and wife should. St. John insists on the marriage. After much discussion, they are unable to overcome the obstacle of the marriage issue, so St. John asks Jane to think about his proposal for a couple of weeks. He warns her that rejecting his proposal means rejecting God.

Commentary

St. John's absolute, God-sanctioned despotism becomes apparent in this chapter. Just as Brocklehurst was a "black pillar," St. John is "a white stone" and a "cold cumbrous column"; Brocklehurst was evil and St. John is good, but both men are equally stony. Even St. John's kisses are "marble" or "ice" kisses: No warmth or affection warms them.

St. John's God is an infallible, warrior deity: king, captain, and law-giver. Similarly, Jane says she would accompany St. John as "comrade" or "fellow-soldier." He uses imagery of war to describe his devotion to this God: He will "enlist" under the Christian "banner," Jane says he prizes her like a soldier would an effective weapon, under God's "standard" St. John "enlists" Jane, and she should "wrench" her heart from humanity to fix it upon God. All of these quotes suggest the violence and severity that underlies St. John's views of Christianity. Like Helen Burns, he has his eyes turned on heaven, but while her spirituality emphasized a martyred compassion, his makes God into a warrior tyrant who demands absolute submission. While Helen sought solace in heaven to compensate for her unhappy life on earth, St. John seeks glory in heaven to make up for his obscurity on earth.

The representation of marriage in this chapter suggests its inherently oppressive nature. St. John argues that a wife would be "the sole helpmeet I can influence efficiently in life, and retain absolutely till death"; thus, he wants a wife he can control completely. Jane recognizes the imperialism in his statement. As his "curate" or "comrade," Jane could preserve her "unblighted" self, but as his wife, she would become "part of" him and, therefore, "always restrained," her flame "imprisoned," perhaps leading to the madness that afflicts Bertha Mason. As husband, St. John would invade the private places in her mind, trample her with his "warrior-march," ultimately erasing her identity and dousing her passions for life. Rather than resisting like the madwoman in the attic, Jane would become a mere husk. Both Rochester and St. John value Jane for her seeming submissiveness, thinking they can shape her into their ideal versions of woman, but her strength surprises them both.

Glossary

paysannes peasant women.

Bäuerinnen peasant women.

beau ideal the perfect type.

carte blanche complete authority.

Chapter 35

Summary

Rather than leaving for Cambridge the next day, St. John delays his trip for a week. During that time, he subtly punishes Jane for not obeying him. Remembering that he once saved her life, Jane tries to reconcile with him, asking him to treat her as a kinswoman, rather than a stranger. She tells him she retains her resolution not to marry him, and adds that he is literally killing her with his icy chill. But her words don't help; instead, they make him hate her. St. John accuses her of breaking her promise of going to India, and Jane invokes the reader's memory, asking us to confirm that she never gave him a formal promise. Before going to India, Jane wants to be certain she couldn't be of greater use in England. St. John recognizes that she refers to Rochester, and tells her she should crush this "lawless and unconsecrated" attachment. He then leaves for a walk.

Recognizing that St. John and Jane have quarreled, Diana discusses the situation with Jane. Diana doesn't think Jane would live three months in India, and urges her to reject St. John's proposal. Like Jane, Diana feels it would be crazy for Jane to chain herself to a man who sees her as nothing but a useful tool. Following dinner that evening, St. John prays for Jane and she feels veneration for his talent and oratorical powers. At this moment, Jane is tempted to yield to his influences and marry him. All the house is quiet, except for St. John and Jane. Suddenly, she feels an electric shock pass through her body, and the words, "Jane! Jane! Jane!" repeated in Rochester's voice. For Jane, this is not superstition, but nature, saving her from a grave error. Now she is able to resist St. John's power.

Commentary

Literary Device

Notice that the imagery in this chapter continues to develop St. John's inhumanity: he is "no longer flesh, but marble"; his eye is "a cold, bright, blue gem"; and his heart seems made of "stone or metal." For Jane, his coldness is more terrible that Rochester's raging; she asks if her readers know the "terror those cold people can put into the ice of their questions? how much of the fall of the avalanche is in their anger? of the breaking up of the frozen sea in their displeasure?" St. John is associated with falling avalanches and the breaking up of frozen seas, natural events that are unpredictable and uncontrollable. Despite St. John's obvious flaws, Diana and Jane continually remind the reader that he is a "good man." This goodness isn't obvious in Jane's depiction of him. For a twenty-first-century reader, even his missionary zeal is morally suspect, because it shows his participation in the colonialist project, which resulted in violence and the violation of native peoples. The goal of this project was to represent native peoples as "savages," in need of British guidance and enlightenment. St. John's coldheartedness suggests the brutality and self-serving function of colonialism. Jane claims St. John "forgets, pitilessly, the feelings and claims of little people, in pursuing his own large views": imagine the damage he will inflict on any native people who resist him; like Jane, they will be "blighted" by his merciless egotism.

Yet Jane is drawn to this merciless man, as if she wants to lose herself. By the end of the chapter, she is tempted to stop struggling with him, and "rush down the torrent of his will into the gulf of his existence, and there lose my own." She is saved, not by her own powers, but by the supernatural. A major change in Jane's life is once again signaled by a psychic event. As she is about to accept St. John's wishes, Jane experiences a sensation as "sharp, as strange, as shocking" as an electric shock. Then she hears Rochester's voice calling her name. So powerful is this voice that Jane cries, "I am coming," and runs out the door into the garden, but she discovers no sign of Rochester. She rejects the notion that this is the devilish voice of witchcraft, but feels it comes from benevolent nature, not a miracle, but nature's best effort to help her—the "universal mother" nurtures Jane again. As during her dark night on the heath, Jane feels the solace of a comforting nature helping and guiding her. She gathers enough force and energy to finally assert her independence from St. John: It is her time to "assume ascendancy." Following this experience, Jane returns to her room to pray in her own way, a way that's different from St. John's, but effective. Jane has already rejected St. John's approach to love, and now she also rejects his way of spirituality. While St. John maintains distance from God, who is always his superior, Jane penetrates "very near a Mighty Spirit; and my soul rushed out in gratitude at His feet"—this spirit, not necessarily the Christian God, provides her with the comfort and peace that St. John never feels.

Chapter 36

Summary

At dawn the next morning, Jane rises. St. John slides a note under Jane's door, reminding her to resist temptation. It is the first of June, yet the day is chilly and overcast. Jane wanders the house, thinking about the previous night's visitation: Was it a delusion? It seemed to come from her, not from the external world. At breakfast, she tells Diana and Mary she'll be away at least four days. She catches a coach at Whitcross, the same one she road from Thornfield a year earlier.

Alighting from the coach, Jane finds herself again on Rochester's lands. She is anxious to see him again and hurries the two miles from the coach stop to the house, worrying that he may be in Europe. Like a lover who wishes to catch a glimpse of his lover's face without waking her, then finds she is "stone dead," Jane is appalled by the sight that awaits her: Thornfield is a blackened ruin. What is the story behind this disaster, Jane wonders? Jane returns to the inn near the coach station, the Rochester Arms, to find an answer. She discovers that Bertha Mason set the house on fire last autumn. Before this happened, Rochester had shut himself up like a hermit in the house, as if he had gone mad. When the fire broke out, Rochester saved the servants, then tried to save Bertha, but she jumped from Thornfield's roof. Rochester has lost his sight and one of his hands in the fire. He now lives in Ferndean with two old servants, John and Mary.

Commentary

Literary Device

Suspense builds in this chapter, as Jane delays the revelation of Thornfield's tragic end and of Rochester's history. Upon entering the coach at Whitcross, Jane reflects on the major changes in her situation since her arrival there a year earlier. Then she was "desolate, and hopeless, and objectless"; now she has friends, hope, and money. Then she paid all the money she had to ride the coach, now she has a secure fortune. Arriving in Thornfield, Jane notices the difference between the scenery here and in Morton (the place she has just left); Thornfield is mild, green, and pastoral, while Morton is stern. Thornfield's landscape is as comfortable as a "once familiar face," whose character she knows intimately. Notice the stark contrast between Jane's comforting, flowering, breathtaking dream of Thornfield and the reality of its trodden and wasted grounds; the world's vision of the upper classes doesn't always capture the hidden passions that boil under the veneer of genteel tranquility. The passions kindling at Thornfield have finally sparked and burned the house down; Rochester's burning bed was merely a prelude. Jane's psychic powers have been reaffirmed as another of her dreams has become reality.

The passions that have burned down Rochester's family mansion, leaving it "a lonesome wild," are, in Jane's version of the story, centered in a woman: Bertha Mason. Jane refuses to recognize her own part in this tale of excessive passion: the innkeeper tries to tell her of Rochester's irresistible love for Jane, which he labels a midlife crisis: "when gentlemen of his age fall in love with girls, they are often like as if they are bewitched." But Jane cuts him off, asking him to tell this part of the story at another time. As simply a specimen of a common phenomenon—midlife crisis—Jane and Rochester's love loses some of its romantic force. In addition, Jane doesn't want to be associated with Thornfield's tragic end, so Bertha Mason becomes the scapegoat. Critics have viewed Bertha as the odious symbol of Rochester's sexual drive; as Jane's double, the angry, repressed side of the orphan child; or as a scapegoat destroyed to redeem Jane. In setting fire to Thornfield, Bertha begins by torching the hangings in the room next to her own, but then kindles Jane's old bed. Her anger seems to focus on sexual jealousy of her rival. During her final rebellion, Bertha stands on the roof Thornfield, "waving her arms above the battlements, and shouting out till they could hear her a mile off," with her long, dark hair "streaming against the flames." The fire becomes a representation of Bertha's power. She is a strong, large, extravagant, and sensual woman, who contrasts with Jane, described by the innkeeper as "a little, small thing . . . almost like a child."

Rochester must pay for the transgression of almost making Jane his mistress. Following her departure from Thornfield, he becomes "savage" and "dangerous," but redeems himself by saving his servants and even trying to rescue his hated wife; as the innkeeper says, Rochester's courage and kindness resulted in his injuries. Unlike her depiction of St. John, which uniformly emphasizes his coldness and domination, Jane peppers her description of Rochester with examples of his compassion and caring.

Chapter 37

Summary

Jane rushes to Ferndean, a building buried deep in the woods. While she watches the building, the door slowly opens, and Rochester reaches out a hand to see if it's raining. She notes that his body hasn't changed, but his face looks "desperate and brooding." After Rochester has returned to the house, Jane knocks on the door. Mary is surprised to see her so late at night and in this lonely place.

Mary is taking a tray with candles and a glass of water to Rochester, and Jane volunteers to carry it instead. As she walks into the parlor, Rochester's dog, Pilot, is excited to see Jane, almost knocking the tray from her hand. Rochester wonders what is wrong. Realizing Jane is in the room with him, Rochester initially thinks she is only a disembodied voice. He grabs her hand, and wraps her in his arms. She assures him she's not a dream and promises to stay with him forever.

The next morning, as they wander through the woods, Jane tells Rochester the story of her experiences during the year they've been apart. Rochester is jealous of St. John Rivers, believing she has fallen in love with her handsome cousin. Jane assures him she could never love the cold and despotic St. John. He proposes to her, and she accepts. Rochester then apologizes for trying to make Jane his mistress; he now regrets that decision. He reveals that four nights earlier, during a low point in his life, he had frantically called Jane's name and thought he heard her answer. Jane doesn't tell him about her similar experience, because she doesn't want to upset him in his weakened state. Rochester thanks God for his mercy, vowing to live a purer life from then on.

Commentary

Jane has now reached her final destination: Ferndean. Her description of Ferndean emphasizes its isolation. It is deep in the woods, unsuitable and unhealthy. Recall that earlier in the novel, Rochester chose not to send Bertha there, because he didn't want her to hasten her death. The woods surrounding the building are thick, dark and gloomy, as if lost in a fairy-tale realm; Jane can barely find an opening through the dense trees to the house. Here, Jane and Rochester create the "private island" he longed for earlier in the novel.

In describing Rochester, Jane uses language Rochester often used in the past to characterize her: he is a "wronged" bird, a "caged eagle." But now their positions are reversed: Jane is free, and he is fettered. In their first conversation, Jane emphasizes her independence: "I am independent, sir, as well as rich: I am my own mistress." While earlier Rochester treated Jane as an object—his possession—he now accepts her independent subjectivity; thus, when he proposes marriage this time he says, "Never mind fine clothes and jewels, now: all that is not worth a fillip." Like Jane, Rochester needed to "pass through the valley of the shadow of death" in order to become the perfect mate; his fire and virility are tamed and he becomes the ideally docile husband. Rochester suffers more than Jane—blinding, maiming, and complete isolation—because his sins were greater than hers. In fact, critics have often noted that both Bertha and Rochester can be viewed as victims of the forces Jane uses to acquire identity and independence; Bertha's life is sacrificed, as well as Rochester's vision, so that Jane can have her ideal, non-threatening relationship.

Ensconced in Ferndean's desolation, the lovers have also achieved spiritual isolation. While Jane emphasizes Rochester's atonement for the sin of trying to make Jane his mistress, she also reminds readers of the ideal telepathic bond between the lovers. This psychic sympathy leads Jane to hear Rochester's frantic call for her, and for Rochester to pick her response out of the wind. In fact, he even correctly intuits that her response came from some mountainous place. Jane cannot find the words to explain this awful coincidence to Rochester: His mind is already dark, and doesn't need the "deeper shade of the supernatural." Yet the reader's mind evidently doesn't suffer the same deficiency as Rochester's, because Jane is happy to share this odd occurrence with her audience. In some sense, Jane seems to be patronizing Rochester here. If their minds are supposedly in "perfect concord," why can't she share this information with Rochester? Although Brontë used this psychic affinity to emphasize the spiritual bond between the lovers, critics have often argued that the novel relies too heavily on coincidence.

Glossary

faux air alse appearance.

jeune encore still young.

Chapter 38

Summary

Rochester and Jane finally marry with a quiet ceremony. Immediately, Jane writes to the Rivers, explaining what she has done. Diana and Mary both approve of her marriage, but Jane receives no response from St. John. Not having forgotten Adèle, Jane visits her at school. The girl is pale, thin, and unhappy, so Jane moves her to a more indulgent school. Adèle grows into a docile, good-natured young woman.

At the writing of this story, Jane has been married for ten years. She feels blessed beyond anything language can express, because she and Rochester love each other absolutely. For two years, Rochester remained almost completely blind, but slowly his sight has returned to him. He was able to see his first-born son. And what has happened to the rest of the cast? Diana and Mary Rivers have both married. St. John is still a missionary in India, but is nearing death. The final words of the novel are his: "Amen; even so, come, Lord Jesus!"

Commentary

The novel has a typically—for a Victorian story—happy ending. All of the characters who were good to Jane are rewarded. Diana and Mary Rivers have made loving marriages; Adèle, not at fault for her mother's sins, has become Jane's pleasing companion. Notice Jane's final ethnocentric comment in relation to little Adèle: "a sound English education corrected in a great measure her French defects." Only through a good English lifestyle has Adèle avoided her mother's tragic flaws—materialism and sensuality—characteristics the novel specifically associates with foreign women. Rochester and Jane have been reunited in a marriage that appears to be perfect: "[n]o woman was ever nearer to her mate than I am: ever more absolutely bone of his bone and flesh of his flesh." While she feared losing herself in a relationship with St. John, she seems perfectly content to become one with Rochester. What are the differences in the relationships; how does Jane maintain her integrity with Rochester? Primarily through his injuries. As his "vision" and "right hand," Jane maintains a sense of dependence over her husband. Thus the chapter blends an odd mix of language designating their "perfect concord" with language showing Rochester's dependence: He sees nature and books through her, for example. Could this relationship have flourished without Rochester's infirmities? For two years of good behavior, Jane grants Rochester partial regeneration of his sight, though he still cannot read or write much.

St. John Rivers has also received his just reward. He toils in India, laboring for "his race." A great warrior, St. John sternly clears the "painful way to improvement" for the natives, slaying *their* prejudices of "creed and caste," though obviously not his own. In his zealous Christianity, he obviously sees the Indians as an inferior race, and hopes to implant British virtues and values in their supposedly deficient minds. Perhaps to the joy of those he disciplines in India, St. John is nearing death. Despite Jane's difficulties with Christianity throughout the novel, St. John's words of longing for heaven end the novel. Telling his "Master" that he comes "quickly," St. John's words to Rochester's disembodied cry: "I am coming; wait for me." Love is still Jane's religion; in relationship, Jane has found her heaven.

CHARACTER ANALYSES

Jane Eyre

The novel charts the growth of Jane Eyre, the first-person narrator, from her unhappy childhood with her nasty relatives, the Reeds, to her blissful marriage to Rochester at Ferndean. Reading, education, and creativity are all essential components of Jane's growth, factors that help her achieve her final success. From the novel's opening chapters to its close, Jane reads a variety of texts: *Pamela*, *Gulliver's Travels*, and *Marmion*. Stories provide Jane with an escape from her unhappy domestic situation, feeding her imagination and offering her a vast world beyond the troubles of her real life: By opening her inner ear, she hears "a tale my imagination created . . . quickened with all incident, life, fire, feeling, that I desired and had not in my actual existence." Similarly, she believes education will allow her the freedom to improve her position in society by teaching her to act like a "lady," but her success at school, in particular her drawing ability, also increases her self-confidence. Jane confesses that artistic creation offers her one of the "keenest pleasures" of her life, and Rochester is impressed with Jane's drawings because of their depth and meaning, not typical of a schoolgirl.

Although artistic and educational pursuits are essential elements of Jane's personality, she also feels a need to assert her identity through rebellion. In the opening chapters of the novel, Jane refers to herself as a "rebel slave," and throughout the story she opposes the forces that prevent her from finding happiness: Mrs. Reed's unfair accusations, Rochester's attempt to make her his mistress, and St. John's desire to transform her into a missionary wife. By falling in love with Rochester, she implicitly mutinies against the dictates of class boundaries that relegate her, as a governess, to a lower status than her "master." Besides rejecting traditional views of class, she also denigrates society's attempts to restrict women's activities. Women, she argues, need active pursuits and intellectual stimulation, just as men do. Most of Jane's rebellions target the inequities of society, but much of her personality is fairly conventional. In fact, she often seems to provide a model of proper English womanhood: frank, sincere, and lacking in personal vanity.

Jane's personality balances social awareness with spiritual power. Throughout the novel, Jane is referred to as an imp, a fairy, a relative of the "men in green." As fairy, Jane identifies herself as a special, magical creature. Connecting herself with the mythical beings in Bessie's stories, Jane is affiliated with the realms of imagination, with the fantastic. Jane's psychic abilities aren't merely imaginary: her dreams and visions have a real impact on her life. For example, supernatural experiences, heralds of visions "from another world," foreshadow drastic changes in Jane's life, such as her move from Gateshead to Lowood, or her rediscovery of Rochester after their time apart. Thus, Jane's spirituality isn't a purely Christian one—in fact, she rejects many of the Christian characters in the novel, such as St. John Rivers, Eliza Reed, and Mr. Brocklehurst—but a mixture of Christian and pagan ideas. Like nature, Jane's God is filled with bounty, compassion, and forgiveness—qualities lacking in many of the spiritual leaders she criticizes in the novel.

Edward Fairfax Rochester

While Jane's life has been fairly sedate, long, quiet years at Lowood, Rochester's has been wild and dissipated. An example of the Byronic hero, Rochester is a passionate man, often guided by his senses rather than by his rational mind. For example, when he first met Bertha Mason, he found her dazzling, splendid, and lavish—all qualities that excited his senses and resulted in their catastrophic marriage. Similarly, he let himself be ruled by his "grande passion" for Céline Varens, despite its immorality. Rochester is not afraid to flout social conventions. This is also apparent in his relationship with Jane: Rather than maintaining proper class boundaries, Rochester makes her feel "as if he were my relation rather than my master."

Like Jane, Rochester is connected with almost psychic powers. His "wealth" of power for communicating happiness seems magical to Jane, as are his abilities to read people's unspoken thoughts from their eyes with incomprehensible acumen. As gypsy fortuneteller, he weaves a magical web around Jane with words and looks directly into her heart so that she feels an "unseen spirit" is watching and recording all of her feelings. He also peers into Blanche's heart, recognizing her for a fortune hunter. Finally, his telepathic cry to Jane when she's at Moor House shows his psychic ability. Like Jane, he taps into the magical powers of the universe in professing his love.

When he meets Jane, Rochester is planning to change his lifestyle. Giving up his wild, dissipated life on the continent, he's searching for freshness and freedom. Rochester's goal is self-transformation, a reformation to be enacted through his relationships with women. Longing for innocence and purity, he wants Jane to be the good angel in his life, creating new harmony. Despite these desires for a new life, Rochester is still caught in a web of lies and immorality: He attempts bigamy and then tries to convince Jane to be his mistress. He also tries to objectify Jane by clothing her in expensive satins and laces, leaving her feeling like a "performing ape." Although Rochester had critiqued Blanche Ingram and Céline Varens for their materialism and superficiality, here he seems to be mimicking them. Rochester's passions and materialism need to be disciplined before he can be the proper husband for Jane. Perhaps not insignificantly, he is blinded and loses a hand when Bertha sets fire to Thornfield; symbolically, his excessive passion has finally exploded, leaving him disabled. Rochester has passed "through the valley of the shadow of death" to become the perfect mate. Having finally paid for his sins, he is now a suitably docile husband for Jane, who morally guides and corrects him at novel's end.

St. John Rivers

While Rochester is a prototype of the fiery, passionate man, St. John Rivers is his opposite: cold, hard-hearted, and repressed. His handsome appearance indicates moral and intellectual superiority—he has "a straight, classic nose; quite an Athenian mouth and chin"—and contrasts with Rochester's more rugged features. Although St. John initially appears perfect, Jane soon detects a restlessness or hardness under his seemingly placid features; he is "no longer flesh, but marble" and his heart seems made of "stone or metal." His reserve and brooding suggest a troubled nature, and his zealous Christianity offers him neither serenity nor solace. St. John's feelings about Christianity are revealed in his sermons, which have a "strictly restrained zeal" that shows his bitterness and hardness. While Rochester vents his passions, St. John represses his. The iciness of St. John's character is most pronounced in his relationship with Rosamond Oliver. Although he "flushes" and "kindles" at the sight of her, St. John would rather turn himself into "an automaton" than succumb to Rosamond's beauty or fortune. His ambition cuts St. John off from all deep human emotions. For Jane, this coldness is more terrible than Rochester's raging; she asks if readers know the "terror those cold people can put into the ice of their questions"?

Not content with his humble local ministry, St. John would like to have been a politician, a poet, or anything that could have offered him glory, fame, and power. His solution is to become a missionary, a position that will require all of these skills. The weakness of his supposed Christianity is his lack of compassion for or interest in the people he is supposedly helping. For him, missionary work isn't about joy, but a form of "warfare" against the prejudices of the natives, just as he "wars" against Jane's rejection of his marriage proposal. Instead of asking her to help him in a mission of love in India, St. John "enlists" Jane to join his band of Christian mercenaries. He wants a wife he can "influence efficiently" and "retain absolutely," rather than someone he loves. Marriage to St. John would traumatically erase Jane's identity and douse her passions for life. St. John achieves his goal and conducts a "warrior-march trample" through India, ultimately dying young following ten hard years of missionary work.

CRITICAL ESSAYS

A Marxist Approach to *Jane Eyre*

Based on the ideas of Karl Marx, this theoretical approach asks us to consider how a literary work reflects the socioeconomic conditions of the time in which it was written. What does the text tell us about contemporary social classes and how does it reflect classism? *Jane Eyre* depicts the strict, hierarchical class system in England that required everyone to maintain carefully circumscribed class positions. Primarily through the character of Jane, it also accents the cracks in this system, the places where class differences were melding in Victorian England. For example, the novel questions the role of the governess: Should she be considered upper class, based on her superior education, or lower class, because of her servant-status within the family? What happens when relationships develop between people of different classes, such as Rochester and Jane?

Jane's ambiguous class status becomes evident from the novel's opening chapter. A poor orphan living with relatives, Jane feels alienated from the rest of the Reed family. John Reed tells Jane she has "no business to take our books; you are a dependent . . . you ought to beg, and not to live here with gentleman's children like us." In this quote, John claims the rights of the gentleman, implying that Jane's family was from a lower class, and, therefore, she has no right to associate on equal footing with her wealthy cousins. Jane's lack of money leaves her dependent upon the Reeds for sustenance. She appears to exist in a no-man's land between the upper- and servant classes. By calling her cousin John a "murderer," "slave-driver," and "Roman emperor," Jane emphasizes her recognition of the corruption inherent in the ruling classes. As she's dragged away to the red-room following her fight with John Reed, Jane resists her captors like a "rebel slave," emphasizing the oppression she suffers because of her class status. When Miss Abbot admonishes Jane for striking John Reed, Jane's "young master," Jane immediately questions her terminology. Is John really her "master"; is she his servant? Emphasizing the corruption, even despotism of the upper classes, Jane's narrative makes her audience aware that the middle classes were becoming the repositories of both moral and intellectual superiority.

Jane's experiences at Thornfield reinforce this message. When Jane first arrives, she is happy to learn that Mrs. Fairfax is a housekeeper, and not Jane's employer, because this means they're both dependents and can, therefore, interact as equals. Mrs. Fairfax discusses the difference between herself, as an upper-servant, and the other servants in the house;

for example, she says Leah and John are "only servants, and one can't converse with them on terms of equality; one must keep them at due distance for fear of losing one's authority." As a governess, Jane is in the same category as Mrs. Fairfax: neither a member of the family nor a member of the serving classes. The ambiguity of the governess is especially pronounced, as we see with the example of Diana and Mary Rivers: the well-educated daughters of upper-class parents who've fallen on hard financial times, the Rivers are better educated than their employers, though treated with as little respect as the family cook. Victorian society brutally maintained the boundaries between governesses and the upper-class families, practically prohibiting marriages between the two groups and attempting to desexualize governesses, who were often accused of bringing a dangerous sexuality into the family. Blanche, for example, calls governesses "incubi," and Lady Ingram believes that liaisons should never be allowed between governesses and tutors, because such relationships would introduce a moral infection into the household.

The relationship between Jane and Rochester also emphasizes class issues. In a conversation preceding their betrothal, Rochester treats Jane like a good servant: Because she's been a "dependent" who has done "her duty," he, as her employer, wants to offer her assistance in finding a new job. Jane confirms her secondary status by referring to Rochester as "master," and believing "wealth, caste, custom," separate her from him. She fears he will treat her like an "automaton" because she is "poor, obscure, plain and little," mistakenly believing the lower classes to be heartless and soulless. Claiming the aristocratic privilege of creating his own rules, Rochester redefines Jane's class status, by defining her as his "equal" and "likeness."

Before she can become Rochester's wife, Jane must prove her acceptability based on class. Does she have an upper-class sensibility, despite her inferior position at Thornfield? For example, when Bessie sees Jane at Lowood, she is impressed because Jane has become "quite a lady"; in fact, her accomplishments surpass that of her cousins, yet they are still considered her social superiors based solely on wealth. The conversation emphasizes the ambiguities of Jane's family's class status and of the class system in general: Should a lady be judged based on academic accomplishments, money, or family name? The novel critiques the behavior of most of the upper-class characters Jane meets: Blanche Ingram is haughty and superficial, John Reed is debauched, and Eliza Reed is inhumanely cold. Rochester is a primary example of upper-class debauchery, with his series of mistresses and his attempt to make Jane a member of the harem. In her final view of Thornfield, after Bertha has burned it down, Jane emphasizes the stark contrast between her comforting, flowering, breathtaking dream of Thornfield, and the reality of its trodden and wasted grounds. The discrepancy emphasizes that the world's vision of the upper classes doesn't always capture the hidden passions that boil under the veneer of genteel tranquility.

One of Jane's tasks in the novel is to revitalize the upper classes, which have become mired in debauchery and haughtiness. Just as Rochester sought Jane for her freshness and purity, the novel suggests that the upper classes in general need the pure moral values and stringent work ethic of the middle classes. At novel's end, Rochester recognizes the error in his lifestyle, and his excessive passions have been quenched; he is reborn as a proper, mild-mannered husband, happily dependent on his wife's moral and intellectual guidance.

A Jungian Approach to *Jane Eyre*

The famous psychologist Carl Jung was interested in *the collective unconscious,* or the primordial images and ideas that reside in every human being's psyche. Often appearing in the form of dreams, visions, and fantasies, these images provoke strong emotions that are beyond the explanation of reason. In *Jane Eyre,* the bounds of reality continually expand, so that dreams and visions have as much validity as reason, providing access to the inner recesses of Jane's and Rochester's psyches. Their relationship also has a supernatural component.

Throughout the novel, Jane is described as a "fairy." Sitting in the red-room, she labels herself a "tiny phantom, half fairy, half imp" from one of Bessie's bedtime stories, a spirit-creature that comes out of "lone, ferny dells in moors." As fairy, Jane identifies herself as a special, magical creature, and reminds the reader of the importance that imagination plays in her life. Jane's dreams have a prophetic character, suggesting their almost supernatural ability to predict the future. In a dream foreshadowing the direction of her relationship with Rochester, she is "tossed on a buoyant but unquiet sea." Jane's dream warns her that their relationship will be rocky, bringing chaos and passion into her life. Similarly, her dreams of infants are prophetic, indicating impending trouble in her life.

Not only is Jane a mythical creature, but the narrative she creates also has a mythic element, mixing realism and fantasy. We see the first instance of this as Jane sits nervously in the red-room and imagines a gleam of light shining on the wall; for her, this indicates a vision "from another world. Generally, supernatural occurrences such as these serve as transition points in the novel, signaling drastic changes in Jane's life. As Jane's departure from Gateshead was marked by her pseudo-supernatural experience in the red-room, her movement away from Lowood also has a paranormal component. Meditating upon the best means for discovering a new job, Jane is visited by a "kind fairy" who offers her a solution. This psychic counselor gives her very specific advice: Place an advertisement in the local newspaper, with answers addressed to J.E., and do it immediately. The fairy's plan works, and Jane soon discovers the job at Thornfield.

As a gypsy woman, Rochester aligned himself with mystical knowledge. During his telling of her fortune, Rochester seems to have peered directly into Jane's heart, leaning her deep into a dream-state she likens to "a web of mystification." He magically weaves a web around Jane with words, and appears to have watched every movement of her heart, like an "unseen spirit." During this scene, he wears a red cloak, showing that he has taken over the position of Red Riding Hood that Jane held earlier. The potion he gives Mason also has mystical powers, giving Mason the strength he lacks for an hour or so, hinting at Rochester's mysterious, possibly supernatural powers.

In emphasizing the uniqueness of Jane and Rochester's love, Brontë gives their meetings a mythical feel, so that they are depicted as archetypes of true lovers. Her association of Rochester's horse and dog with the mythical Gytrash places their initial meeting in an almost fairytale-like setting. Later, Rochester reveals that at this initial meeting, he thought Jane was a fairy who had bewitched his horse, and he repeatedly refers to her as a sprite or elfin character, claiming the "men in green" are her relatives. The lovers' reunion at the end of the novel also has a psychic component. As she is about to accept St. John's wishes, Jane experiences a sensation as "sharp, as strange, as shocking" as an electric shock. Then she hears Rochester's voice call her name. The voice comes from nowhere, speaking "in pain and woe, wildly, eerily, urgently." So powerful is this voice that Jane cries, "I am coming," and runs out the door into the garden, but she discovers no sign of Rochester. She rejects the notion that this is the devilish voice of witchcraft, but feels that it comes from benevolent nature; not a miracle, but nature's best effort to help her, as if the forces of nature are assisting this very special relationship. She introduces the ideal of a telepathic bond between the lovers. This psychic sympathy leads Jane to hear Rochester's frantic call for her, and for Rochester to pick her response out of the wind. In fact, he even correctly intuits that her response came from some mountainous place. Through the novel's supernatural elements, Jane and Rochester become archetypes of ideal lovers, supporting Jane's exorbitant claim that no one "was ever nearer to her mate than I am." These mythic elements transform their relationship from ordinary to extraordinary.

A Postcolonial Approach to *Jane Eyre*

As a theoretical approach, postcolonialism asks readers to consider the way colonialist and anti-colonialist messages are presented in literary texts. It argues that Western culture is Eurocentric, meaning it presents European values as natural and universal, while Eastern ideas are, for example, inferior, immoral, or "savage." A postcolonial approach to *Jane Eyre* might begin by considering the following questions: What does the novel reveal about the way cultural difference was represented in Victorian culture? How did Britain justify its colonialist project by imaging the East as "savage" or uncivilized? What idea does the text create of "proper" British behavior? Tentative answers to these questions can be discovered by examining the novel's representation of foreign women, especially Bertha Mason, and the colonialist doctrines of Jane and of St. John Rivers.

One of the colonialist goals of this novel is to create a prototype of the proper English woman, someone like Jane who is frank, sincere, and lacking in personal vanity. This ideal is created by Jane's attempt to contrast herself with the foreign women in the text. For example, both Céline Varens and her daughter are constantly criticized in the novel for their supposed superficiality and materialism. According to Rochester, Céline Varens charmed the "English gold" out of his "British breeches," a comment that emphasizes his supposedly British innocence and her wily French ways. Supporting this idea, Jane comments that Adèle has a superficiality of character, "hardly congenial to an English mind." Jane's final ethnocentric comments in relation to little Adèle are significant: "a sound English education corrected in a great measure her French defects." Only through a good English lifestyle has Adèle avoided her mother's tragic flaws: materialism and sensuality, characteristics the novel specifically associates with foreign women. Jane's comments imply that the English, unlike their French neighbors, are deep rather than superficial, spiritual rather than materialistic.

But Jane's position is more conflicted than Rochester's: As a woman she is also a member of a colonized group, but as a specifically British woman, she is a colonizer. When she claims Rochester gives her a smile such as a sultan would "bestow on a slave his gold and gems had enriched," she emphasizes the colonized status of all women. Insisting that he prefers his "one little English girl" to the "Grand Turk's whole seraglio," Rochester points to Jane's powerlessness, her reduction to sex slave. Rather than becoming slave, Jane insists she will become a missionary, preaching liberty to women enslaved in harems. Her comments show the dual position of European women: both colonized and colonizers. While Rochester reduces her to a colonized "doll" or "performing ape," her comments show her Eurocentric understanding of Eastern culture: She implies that she'll be the enlightened Englishwoman coming to the rescue of poor, abused Turkish women. All women are enslaved by male despotism, but the British woman claims a moral and spiritual superiority over her Eastern sisters.

This difference becomes intense in Jane's representation of Bertha Mason. Bertha's vampiric appearance suggests she is sucking the lifeblood away from the innocent Rochester, who tells Jane he was as innocent as she is until he turned twenty-one and was married to Bertha: His goodness was taken by this savage woman. An insane Creole woman, Bertha represents British fears of both foreigners and women. The "blood-red" moon, a symbol of women's menstrual cycles, is reflected in her eyes, suggesting her feminine, sexual potency. Unlike Jane, Bertha refuses to be controlled; a woman whose stature almost equals her husband's, she fights with him, displaying a "virile" force that almost masters Rochester. Post-colonial critics argue that Bertha, the foreign woman, is sacrificed so that British Jane can achieve self-identity. Their arguments suggest Rochester isn't as innocent as he claims; as a colonialist, he was in the West Indies to make money and to overpower colonized men and women. Notice how both Jane and Rochester emphasize his ability to control Bertha's brother, Richard. Much of Rochester's critique of Bertha hinges on her sexuality and exotic excess. When he first met her, Rochester's senses were aroused by her dazzle, splendor, and lusciousness. But he later found her debauchery to be his "Indian Messalina's attribute." Thus, the characteristics that first attract her to him, her sensual excesses, soon repulse him.

The representation of Bertha presents native peoples in the colonies as coarse, lascivious, and ignorant, thus justifying St. John's missionary role: Bertha is a foreign "savage" in need of British guidance and enlightenment. Just as Jane retrains the minds of her lower-class students in England, St. John will reform the values of the pagans in India. Both characters perpetuate a belief in British, Christian-based moral and spiritual superiority. But St. John's inability to "renounce his wide field of mission warfare" shows that his colonialist impulse isn't based on compassion or mutual understanding, but on violence—violating the minds of native peoples, if not their bodies. For twenty-first-century readers, St. John's missionary zeal is morally suspect, because it shows his participation in the colonialist project, which resulted in violence against and violation of native peoples. St. John's coldheartedness suggests the brutality and self-serving function of colonialism. Jane claims St. John "forgets, pitilessly, the feelings and claims of little people, in pursing his own large views"; imagine the damage he will inflict on any native people who resist him. Like Jane, they will be repressed by his merciless egotism. St. John spends the rest of his life laboring for "his race" in India. A great warrior, St. John sternly clears the "painful way to improvement" for the natives, slaying their prejudices of "creed and caste," though obviously not his own. In his zealous Christianity, he sees the Indians as an inferior race and hopes to implant British values in their supposedly deficient minds.

CliffsNotes Review

Use this CliffsNotes Review to test your understanding of the original text, and reinforce what you've learned in this book. After you work through the essay questions and useful practice projects, you're well on your way to understanding a comprehensive and meaningful interpretation of *Jane Eyre*.

Fill in the Blank

1. Jane is a student at _____ School.

2. Jane refuses _____'s marriage proposal because they don't love each other.

3. While at the Reeds', Jane has a fainting spell after she is locked in the _____.

4. Miss Temple leaves Lowood when she _____.

5. Adèle Varens is Rochester's _____.

6. Jane saves Rochester's life when _____ sets fire to the curtains near his bed.

7. Diana and Mary Rivers are _____'s cousins.

8. Jane leaves Moor House after she hears a voice calling, _____.

9. Thornfield is destroyed by a _____.

10. Jane leaves Lowood, looking for "a new _____."

Answers: (1) Lowood. (2) St. John. (3) red-room. (4) gets married. (5) ward. (6) Bertha. (7) Jane's. (8) "Jane, Jane, Jane." (9) fire. (10) servitude.

Identify the Quote

1. "The next thing I remember is waking up with a feeling as if I had had a frightful nightmare, and seeing before me a terrible red glare, crossed with thick black bars. I heard voices, too, speaking with a hollow sound, and as if muffled by a rush of wind or water: agitation, uncertainty, and an all-predominating sense of terror confused by faculties. Ere long, I became aware that some one was handling me; lifting me up and supporting me in a sitting posture, and that more tenderly than I had ever been raised or upheld before. I rested my head against a pillow or an arm, and felt easy."

2. "I see you laugh rarely; but you laugh very merrily; believe me, you are not naturally austere, any more than I am naturally vicious. The Lowood constraint still clings to you somewhat; controlling your features, muffling your voice, and restricting your limbs; and you fear in the presence of a man and a brother—or father, or master, or what you will—to smile too gaily, speak too freely, or move too quickly: but in time, I think you will be natural with me, as I find it impossible to be conventional with you; and then your looks and movements will have more vivacity and variety than they dare offer now. I see at intervals the glance of a curious sort of bird through the close-set bars of a cage: a vivid, restless, resolute captive is there; were it but free, it would soar cloud-high."

3. "Madam," he pursued, "I have a Master to serve whose kingdom is not of this world: my mission is to mortify in these girls the lusts of the flesh, to teach them to clothe themselves with shamefacedness and sobriety, not with braided hair and costly apparel . . . ."

4. "My dearest, don't mention governesses; the word makes me nervous. I have suffered a martyrdom from their incompetency and caprice. I thank Heaven I have now done with them!"

5. "I am the servant of an infallible Master. I am not going out under human guidance, subject to the defective laws and erring control of my feeble fellow-worms: my king, my lawgiver, my captain, is the all-perfect. It seems strange to me that all round me do not burn to enlist under the same banner—to join in the same enterprise."

Answers: (1) Jane Eyre. (2) Mr. Rochester. (3) Mr. Brocklehurt. (4) Dowager Lady Ingram. (5) St. John Rivers.

Essay Questions

1. Explain the importance of paranormal experiences in the novel. What do the characters learn from dreams and visions? How do these experiences modify your understanding of the characters? How do the supernatural elements interact with the novel's realism?

2. Discuss the representations of the various women in the novel: Mrs. Reed, Miss Temple, Céline Varens, Blanche Ingram, Bertha Mason, and Diana and Mary Rivers. What does Jane learn about proper feminine behavior from these women? Which are positive role models? Negative?

3. Explore Jane's ideas of religion. What does she learn about Christianity from Helen Burns, Mr. Brocklehurst, and St. John Rivers? How do their views of Christianity contrast with hers? What problems does she see in their values?

4. Discuss two scenes that show the ambiguity of Jane's social class. What are Jane's opinions of the upper classes and the lower classes? What does the novel say about the social class system in England? Does Brontë critique the system or support it?

5. The narrator in the novel is an older Jane remembering her childhood. Find a few places where the voice of the older Jane intrudes on the narrative. What is the effect of this older voice's intrusions on the story? Does it increase or decrease your sympathy for the young Jane?

6. Jane gives descriptions of several of her paintings and drawings. Why are these artistic renditions important? What do they reveal about Jane's imagination? About her inner self?

7. Discuss the contrast between images of ice and fire in the novel. What moral attributes are associated with fire and with ice? How is this image pattern used to reveal personality? For example, which characters are associated with fire and which with ice? Does Jane achieve balance between fire and ice?

8. Analyze the importance of the five major places Jane lives on her journey: Gateshead, Lowood, Thornfield, Moor House/Marsh End, and Ferndean. What do their names signify? What lessons does Jane learn at each place? Jane provides detailed descriptions of the natural world around each place: What do these descriptions reveal about their character?

9. Compare and contrast Rochester and St. John Rivers. What are their strengths and weaknesses? Why does Jane choose Rochester over St. John?

10. Discuss the representation of foreigners in the novel—Bertha and Richard Mason, Céline and Adèle Varens. How are the colonies represented? What is the source of Rochester's wealth? Of Jane's inheritance?

Practice Projects

1. Create your own renditions of Jane's drawings based on her descriptions of them. Do your drawings help you understand their meaning in new ways?

2. Write a short sequel to the novel, describing Jane and Rochester's married life. What happens to their children? What happens to Jane after she finishes this novel? You could also write alternative endings for the novel: What if Jane had married St. John, for example?

3. As a precursor to studying the text, research Charlotte Brontë's life and culture, exploring the politics, religion, and daily life of Victorian England. What was life like in Brontë's time? What would a normal day be for a teenager?

4. If your school has access to electronic discussion boards or an asynchronous discussion forum such as *TopClass* or *Web Crossing*, post questions and responses as you read through the text. Post a minimum number of questions (two, perhaps) and a minimum number of thoughtful replies (say, four). Try to give fuller, more developed discussion responses instead of a brief response such as "I couldn't agree more."

5. Keep a dialectical reading journal as you read *Jane Eyre*. Purchase dialectical notebook paper (or make it by dividing paper they already have into two columns [the left about 3½ inches, the right about 5 inches] running the length of their paper. In the right column, keep track of the plot (being sure to put in chapter numbers so you can quickly locate passages for class discussion). In the smaller column, write your responses to what you have just read. For instance, you may offer up commentary or questions regarding a particular chapter's action. Working dialectically helps you engage with the text and read actively, rather than passively.

6. Using an electronic search engine such as Yahoo! or Alta Vista, onduct a search for Web sites related to the novel. Assemble a list of sites, critically annotating each one with a few sentences (not just summarizing its content, but really considering the credibility of each site). Create a master list of Web sources, and then make your own Web site for *Jane Eyre*. In lieu of summarizing action, you can discuss film adaptations, research critical approaches to the text and present your findings, discuss visual representations of the text (for example, you can scan drawings and engravings that have accompanied various printed versions of the text, analyzing which themes and ideas the artworks provide), start a discussion board, and so on.

7. Watch a variety of film adaptations of *Jane Eyre*. Look for specific comparisons and contrasts between the films (such as how Rochester and Jane's love is depicted in the text and in the movie; outright deviations from the text; how music, settings, and costumes contribute to our understanding of the novel; the characterization of Blanche Ingram, and so on). Post your findings to a Web site or discussion board on the novel.

CliffsNotes Resource Center

The learning doesn't need to stop here. CliffsNotes Resource Center shows you the best of the best—links to the best information in print and online about the author and/or related works. And don't think that this is all we've prepared for you; we've put all kinds of pertinent information at www.cliffsnotes.com. Look for all the terrific resources at your favorite bookstore or local library and on the Internet. When you're online, make your first stop www.cliffsnotes.com where you'll find more incredibly useful information about Jane Eyre.

Books and Articles

This CliffsNotes book, published by IDG Books Worldwide, Inc., provides a meaningful interpretation of Jane Eyre. If you are looking for information about the author and/or related works, check out these other publications:

EAGLETON, TERRY. *Myths of Power: A Marxist Study of the Brontës*. London: Macmillan, 1975. Eagleton analyzes the conflict between rebellion and conventionality in the Brontë's work, which he believes paralleled contemporary discord between landowners and the working classes. In his analysis of Jane Eyre, Eagleton suggests that at the end of the novel Jane has power over Rochester, who is the novel's sacrificial offering the social conventions.

GILBERT, SANDRA M., AND SUSAN GUBAR. "A dialogue of Self and Soul: Plain Jane's Progress." Chapter 10 of *The Madwoman in the Attic: The Woman Writer and the Nineteenth-Century Literary Imagination*. New Haven: Yale UP, 1979. 336–71. A classic feminist approach to the novel, this essay views Jane's self-discovery as a mythic quest on the order of Bunyan's *Pilgrim's Progress*. Bertha is Jane's double, the ferocious secret self that Jane tries to repress, while Diana and Mary represent the ideal female strength Jane searches for. At Ferndean, Rochester and Jane are finally equals.

HOEVELER, DIANE LONG AND LISA JADWIN. *Charlotte Brontë*. New York: Twayne, 1997. This text provides a biography of Brontë, an extensive annotated bibliography, and insightful critical interpretations of each of her works. The essay on Jane Eyre gives information on the novel's publication and early reception and offers critical readings from three perspectives: formalist, political, and psychoanalytic.

HOEVELER, DIANE LONG AND BETH LAU, eds. *Approaches to Teaching Jane Eyre*. New York: Modern Language Association Press, 1993. A collection of 20 essays that offer a variety of fresh approaches to teaching the novel. The volume includes useful background information, recommended student reading, reference works, and critical commentary.

RHYS, JEAN. *Wide Sargasso Sea*. New York: Norton, 1966. Rhys' imaginative prequel to *Jane Eyre*, this novel imaginatively explores the youth and marriage of Antoinette Bertha Cosway, the madwoman in Rochester's attic. The novel vividly depicts West Indian racial tensions and Rochester's cold-blooded domination over Antoinette.

SPIVAK, GAYATRI. "Three Women's Texts and a Critique of Imperialism." *Critical Inquiry* 12 (1985): 243-61. Suggest the necessity of remembering imperialism when reading nineteenth-century texts. Analyzing *Wide Sargasso Sea* and *Frankenstein* along with *Jane Eyre*, Spivak argues that the novel's imperialism undercuts its message of feminist equality.

It's easy to find books published by IDG Books Worldwide, Inc. You'll find them in your favorite bookstores (on the Internet and at a store near you). We also have three Web sites that you can use to read about all the books we publish:

- www.cliffsnotes.com
- www.dummies.com
- www.idgbooks.com

Internet

Check out these Web resources for more information about *Jane Eyre* and Charlotte Brontë:

Jane Eyre, http://www.way.peachnet.edu/faculty/tstrick/00Spring/Jane_Eyre.html—offers a link to the full text of Elizabeth Gaskell's *The Life of Charlotte Brontë*. Possibly its most unique features are the Power Point slide shows it offers, which could be useful for classroom presentations. Topics of these shows include, "Jane Eyre: An Introduction" and "Jane Eyre: Motifs, Views, and Themes."

The Victorian Web: Jane Eyre, http://landow.stg.brown.edu/victorian/bronte/cbronte/eyreov.html—may provide the most extensive listing of critical essays on the novel available on the Web. Easy-to-navigate, the site offers essays analyzing the novel's themes, imagery, setting, genre, gender relations, religious beliefs, and visual arts. This site links to the Victorian Web's general Charlotte Brontë site. Students may also want to check out the home page, which offers extensive scholarship in Victorian studies.

A Jane Eyre Discussion Board, `http://www.insidetheweb.com/mbs/cgi/mb226432`—allows readers to enter a threaded discussion devoted to the novel and the Brontës.

The Brontë Sisters, `http://www2.sbbs.se/hp/cfalk/bronteng.htm`—offers links to information on each of the Brontë sisters. The Jane Eyre page provides links offering comparisons between Jane Eyre and several other texts, such as *Alice's Adventure's in Wonderland* and *Great Expectations*.

Jane Eyre Appreciation Page, `http://members.tripod.com/~Athenalris/jane.html`—devoted to everything related to Brontë's classic novel, offering movie posters, movie stills, and other pictures from productions of *Jane Eyre*. It also offers insight on the characters of Jane and Rochester.

Victoria Turvey's Jane Eyre Page, `http://www.vturvey.free serve.co.uk/JaneEyre.htm`—subtitled, "a page to celebrate the novel," this site offers numerous links to novel- and Brontë-related sites, a discussion list, and message board. It also looks at Timothy Dalton and Zelah Clarke's portrayals of Rochester and Jane in the 1983 BBC production of the novel.

Next time you're on the Internet, don't forget to drop by `www.cliffsnotes.com`. We've created an online Resource Center that you can use today, tomorrow, and beyond.

Index